Business English
In A Week

Thomas Coskeran has taught economics in business schools for over 20 years, most recently at the University of Durham. He has been an economic adviser to both HM Treasury and the UK's National Health Service and has worked with business to apply economic ideas to tackling the effects of radon, a naturally occurring gas that can cause lung cancer.

He has four daughters, who constantly challenge his thinking on economics.

To Helen, Louise, Sarah and Siobhán, for keeping me off the straight and narrow.

Business Economics In A Week

Thomas Coskeran

Also available in ebook

Contents

Introduction

The defining economic event of recent times – the global financial crisis of 2008 – was good for economists. That might sound crass but the truth is it stimulated interest in the subject by showing how important economic concerns are to our lives. Get the economy wrong and things we take for granted start to fall apart. It's a lesson that applies especially to those working in business, who, more than most, need to understand the subject; a sentiment with which, as you are reading this, you probably agree.

If that's so, then this book aims to help you by:

● showing how economics can be useful for you in business
● explaining economic ideas you might not have had time to explore previously
● stimulating an interest in economics that encourages you to further study.

In the book, I've stuck to presenting ideas sometimes called orthodox economics. There's a healthy tradition in economics of alternative approaches that question this mainstream, but limitations on space mean I haven't explored them. Instead, I have referred to enough controversies between economists on specific topics to help you realize that the economist's universe isn't always harmonious.

Of course, for many that is the subject's attraction. A lack of clear-cut prescriptions on a topic might disappoint, but it also offers opportunities. It means, for example, that you, as a player in the economic game the book discusses, can ask yourself: does what economists say chime with my experience? If it does not, you have every right to comment critically.

The book's structure follows that of the 'In A Week' series, which supposes you'll read a chapter a day over the course of one week. This pattern is particularly useful for our purposes.

Reflecting overnight on what you've read will give you the chance to think about (and question) ideas you've met in a chapter, a process that attempting the 'fact-check' questions at the end of each chapter will assist. You'll also get more out of subsequent discussions, in which I've assumed that you, as the reader, have mastered previous subjects before continuing.

My opening comment above might suggest that economists are unrepentant about the global financial crisis. So let's be clear: it was embarrassing. We didn't identify the underlying problems until too late. But if this failure confirms anything, it's that economics constantly requires new people to take it up. They're the ones who question existing approaches in the subject and bring new insights to it based on their understandings and experiences.

My greatest hope for this book is that it motivates you to further study that brings you to a point where you provide insights that ensure we never experience another crisis like that of 2008. But even if you're not that person, I do hope, once you've finished the book, that you'll have learned things of value to you in your working life, that your understanding of economics and its ways has improved, and, above all, that you'll have enjoyed reading it.

Thomas Coskeran

Economics and your business

Most people's rough idea of economics is that it's about money, or banks, or taxes, or bankrupt businesses and workers who have lost jobs and must find work elsewhere. Economists worry about these problems, so people's rough ideas are roughly right. But to list topics that interest economists does not tell us why economics exists as a subject, what economists do, or how knowledge of economics is helpful. Today is about those questions.

In addressing them, we'll consider two features of life that should match your own experience:

- People's wants are unlimited or infinite. They're never satisfied with what they have, and always want more. I know that's not you, but everybody else seems like that.
- The world's resources are limited such that people's unlimited wants cannot all be satisfied. There is only so much to go round.

Human societies must therefore choose which wants to satisfy. That requires a system – the economy. Economists study how this system works to make the choices the combination of unlimited wants and limited resources require.

So that's today's agenda. Let's get to it!

> *'The ideas of economists and political philosophers, both when they are right and when they are wrong, are more powerful than is commonly understood. Indeed, the world is ruled by little else. Practical men, who believe themselves to be quite exempt from any intellectual influence, are usually the slaves of some defunct economist.'*
>
> John Maynard Keynes

Making choices

It's Sunday. You could be working. After all, many people are: in supermarkets, restaurants and cinemas, in hospitals and fire stations. If only you hadn't started reading this book. But that's life – or so economists think. You can't do everything you want. You must choose from possibilities at your disposal – even on a Sunday.

Choosing one option, though, means giving up alternatives. Today you could have watched a football match on TV or gone shopping. But you didn't. You're reading this book. That's your best alternative. It must be. It's what you're doing. Your next best alternative – what you would be doing if you weren't reading this book – is the opportunity cost of your choice.

What you pay in money when you buy something is usually called the cost. But economists are not that interested in this money cost. It only interests them because it identifies opportunity cost. If a business bought a new machine costing £60,000, we know the business could have bought many other things with that money. The best alternative among them is the opportunity cost of the machine. And that reminds economists why we have a subject called economics.

> ## Work and leisure
>
> An opportunity cost to which economists often refer relates to time. When we work, we give up leisure time, and vice versa. These are opportunity costs. We'll keep coming back to this particular trade-off, as economists like to call it.

Why economics?

Economists think that every human being (including you and me) has unlimited or infinite wants. However much people have, they want more. The trouble is, the world's resources are finite. There aren't enough to satisfy those infinite wants. Instead, there's scarcity: wants exceed available resources. This is the economic problem that implies choices must be made about:

- **what** to produce
- **how** to produce
- **who** gets what
- **when** they get it.

Economists study how these choices are made.

Opportunity cost reminds us of scarcity. It emphasizes that we gave up something to get what we have. If resources weren't scarce, we could have it all and there would be no opportunity cost. But, as your parents probably told you many times, you cannot have everything. That's the world economists inhabit – and everybody else, too.

> ## Infinite wants
>
> Infinite wants help create the economic problem. But they have a positive side. There's always something to do. If wants are infinite, work must be infinite to satisfy them. If anybody tells you unemployment is inevitable, they've not heard about infinite wants.

Economics and business

If economists are honest with themselves, they can have a low reputation among businesspeople. Obviously, that's not you or you would not be reading this book. But for many people, and not just those in in business, economists can seem over-concerned (even obsessed) with theories unrelated to the 'real world'. Faced with fanciful theory or hard-headed pragmatism, there's no contest for most people.

So let's be clear. Economic theories, of which we will meet a few in this book, are not meant to describe reality. Everyone accepts that, even economists. But economists think that they help us understand reality. Good theories ignore real-world complexities and concentrate on what's important about the world.

Take an example. Economists, like many people, think that, if a good becomes cheaper, more people buy it. But this is a simplifying theory. Businesses know that sales of a good depend on more than price: they are also about quality, availability, fashion and so on. The theory identifies just one important reason goods sell. It allows us, though, to predict what happens when prices change. And that's useful.

This simple case shows how economists work. Economics is a 'method of thinking' (theories). In any situation, economists aim to apply the correct theory from the many they have available, so that they understand it better. And understanding the situation means that economists can both predict the future and suggest how to shape it for the better.

The business environment

This, you might think, is all very well, but how does it concern businesses? The reason is the business environment. Businesses, whether big or small, global or local, public or private, must consider what happens beyond their organization.

The acronym PESTLE reminds them of this environment.

P the political environment: central and local government; the European Union (EU)
E the economic environment: our concern!
S the social environment: customs, fashion, attitudes
T the technological environment: new techniques and ways of organizing production
L the legal environment: the rules governments set to regulate businesses
E the natural environment or ecology: resources such as oil, fisheries, clean air and rivers

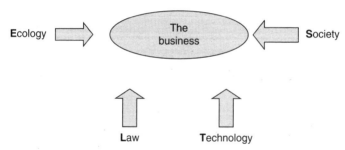

The business environment

The idea of the business environment shows that:

● business activity is constrained
● businesses can, though, campaign to change it
● different elements might oppose one another and create conflicting pressures
● managing these differing pressures, and anticipating them, is crucial for businesses.

Businesses sometimes conduct PESTLE analyses. These involve auditing all elements of the environment to discover how a business might adjust its future strategies to a changing environment.

The economic environment

This book concentrates on the economic environment but PESTLE reminds us that it's only one part of the overall business environment. That's a good lesson for economists. Understanding economics alone doesn't guarantee business success. Running a business involves more. But successful businesspeople would accept – if only on condition of anonymity – that knowing some economics helps them. In short, you need economic knowledge in business but it isn't enough on its own.

Positive and normative

Economists like to think that they use scientific methods and make statements about the economy based on data and suitable theories. For example, they might say: 'Cutting the price of butter increases the quantity of butter demanded.' This is a positive statement.

In contrast, normative statements reflect opinions. For example: 'We should cut the price of butter.' The statement is what somebody believes to be right.

Economists try to avoid normative statements in their work. But sometimes they cannot help themselves and make the normative seem positive. Beware of this tendency.

Economic systems

Societies need an economic system to address the economic problem and ensure they make best use of available resources when executing the choices scarcity requires. Economists try to understand the system, predict what happens in it, and suggest how to improve it.

Economists identify two main systems: the market economy and the planned or command economy. They are ideal types. Neither exists. Instead, they provide a framework for analysing actual economies.

In market economies, prices are central. At the risk of offending you, here's a definition of price: the value, usually expressed in money, of a good or service. In market economies, prices denote scarcity. The higher the price, the scarcer the good. Prices are a barrier to people obtaining goods so only if people really want a good will they pay for it. As prices increase, fewer people want the good. That's how prices allocate scarce resources.

We all have some idea how market economies work from our daily experience and could probably describe it. But economists want to go beyond that and understand what determines prices. We'll examine how they do that tomorrow but for now just say it's supply and demand – or market forces as they are sometimes called.

The market economy: some aliases

The market economy goes under different names depending on context. Karl Marx, a socialist, called it 'capitalism'. Friedrich Hayek, a fan of markets, talked of the 'free market' and 'free enterprise'. Others call it the price mechanism, which recognizes the importance of prices in how it works. And some get familiar and just call it 'the market'.

Markets: an overview

Microeconomics is the part of economics that studies how individuals make decisions and how markets work. As such it is useful for businesses wishing to understand their environment and how their customers behave.

It teaches that in markets:

- producers supply goods and services to make maximum profits (money from sales *minus* costs)
- consumers (customers) demand goods and services to maximize 'satisfaction'
- producers organize factors of production ('factors', for short) to produce goods and services

- factors are land, labour, capital and enterprise (or entrepreneur)
- households own these factors.

Businesses – or firms, as economists sometimes call them – are important producers of goods and services in the economy. They aren't, though, alone. Central and local governments, charities and non-profit organizations all produce for consumers.

As producers, businesses gather together (that's the enterprise) raw materials (land) and machinery (capital) so that workers (labour) in the business can produce products, whether goods or services. These satisfy consumer wants, which, economists think, is the purpose of production.

Each factor receives a reward:

Reward		Factor
Rent	⇨	Land
Wages	⇨	Labour
Interest	⇨	Capital
Profit	⇨	Enterprise (the entrepreneur)

Society must choose how these rewards are divided among the four factors. As we will see on Tuesday, markets can do this.

Although businesses 'consume' when they buy raw materials, machinery and so on from other businesses, or when employing workers, economists usually think consumers are people like you and me who buy stuff. When we do this, economists think that we are out to get satisfaction or utility. It's the feeling we get from consuming a good: the taste and smell of Prosecco! And we want to maximize this satisfaction just as producers want to maximize their profits.

Even though businesses and consumers try to maximize, they both do so subject to constraints. For businesses, it's technology and the cost of the factors they use in production. For consumers, it's their income and the prices they pay for the goods they consume. Both are limited in what they can do. Constraints remind individuals, whether producers or consumers, of scarcity and the need to make choices.

Money in markets

Putting these ideas together, it turns out that the market economy is a perpetual motion machine:

1 Owners of factors of production receive their money rewards.
2 They use the money, as consumers, to buy goods and services from businesses.
3 Businesses use the money they acquire from selling to consumers to employ factors of production.
4 Owners of facto– ... but you see where this is going.

It's called the circular flow of income. This diagram portrays it:

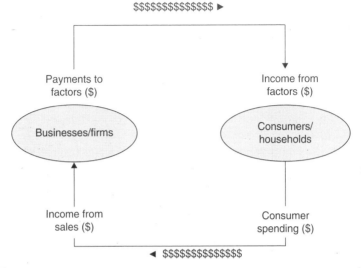

Income flows in the market economy

The diagram also illustrates an important principle. Business spending – paying wages, say, to workers – is income for workers. And when consumers spend, that's income for businesses. At all times, one person's income is another's spending.

Planned and mixed economies

In planned economies, governments decide what, how and when to produce, and who receives what. The Soviet Union ran this type of economy until it fell apart in the 1980s. But the planned economy survives. It's alive and hearty whenever governments involve themselves in the economy. And in all countries, without exception, governments involve themselves in the economy – providing services such as health care, education and a police force.

In reality, all economies are mixed. They are partly market and partly planned, differing only in the share each takes. The spectrum below shows where some national economies lie

between the ideal types economists identify. None is at one of
the two extremes.

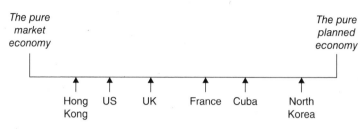

A spectrum of economies

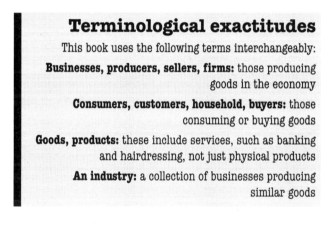

Terminological exactitudes

This book uses the following terms interchangeably:

Businesses, producers, sellers, firms: those producing
goods in the economy

Consumers, customers, household, buyers: those
consuming or buying goods

Goods, products: these include services, such as banking
and hairdressing, not just physical products

An industry: a collection of businesses producing
similar goods

Governments

Governments might provide goods but they also determine
the economy's rules. Businesses, and others, must comply
with laws governing economic behaviour. In some economies,
international organizations lay down laws, too, as the EU does
for member countries. It means that the economic and legal
environments overlap.

Without rules, economies falter. Buyers and sellers must
be confident that they won't be cheated or that, if they are,
they have somewhere to complain. So as well as making
laws, governments provide prosecutors, courts and prisons to
ensure that those laws are enforced.

As in sport, economies need a referee. Governments are the market's referees. But the analogy isn't perfect. Governments referee the economic game, but they also play in it when they produce and consume goods.

To summarize, the economic environment for businesses is neither pure market nor pure planned economy but a mixture of the two, regulated by a government. The rest of this book considers how it works.

Useful economic concepts

Economics gives businesses more than just an understanding of the economic environment. Economists have over the years developed ideas that business can use to improve performance. These ideas, used regularly throughout this book, are the margin, the cost–benefit principle, transaction costs and incentives.

The margin: what happens when things change

Suppose a car manufacturer increases output by one car and costs rise by £5,000. That's the marginal cost of the car. Average cost is the total cost the business incurs divided by total output. If the business produced 10,000 cars and it cost £80 million to produce them, the average cost of a car is £8,000.

Economists think that the margin is more important than the average. If businesses focus on the margin, they can spot profitable opportunities they might otherwise miss.

For example, in the case above, were our car manufacturer offered £6,000 to produce an extra car, it would refuse the offer based on average cost. But 'at the margin', an extra car earns profit of £1,000. Life is never quite this simple, but the principle is.

The cost–benefit principle: making decisions by comparing costs and benefits

We used this idea in the previous example. At the margin, our car manufacturer decides to sell the car as the benefit from selling (£6,000) outweighs the cost of producing (£5,000).

An important tool that applies this principle is cost-benefit analysis. Governments use it to decide whether to pursue major projects such as new roads. In these cases they consider every cost and benefit, not just the monetary. For example, when building roads they estimate the number of accidents that will be avoided. See https://www.gov.uk/government/publications/the-green-book-appraisal-and-evaluation-in-central-governent, for more on how the UK government does this.

An inarticulate economist interviewed

Interviewer: Thanks for discussing economics with us. I'll begin with an important question: Is economics a science?

Economist: No.

Interviewer: Is it a social science?

Economist: Yes.

Interviewer: Does that mean economists apply scientific principles to study human behaviour?

Economist: Yes.

Interviewer: So it's like subjects such as sociology, anthropology, criminology and psychology?

Economist: Yes.

Interviewer: Why isn't economics an -ology?

Economist: Dunno.

Interviewer: What about politics? That's a social science but not an -ology.

Economist: Yes.

Interviewer: Well, thank you for your time and for clearing up the question of whether economics is a science.

Economist: No need to thank me. Just pay me, please. I've given up leisure time to speak to you so you must compensate me for my time spent on this interview. I value it at £33.58. Payment by cash, cheque or credit transfer is fine. I don't accept credit or debit cards.

Transaction costs: the costs of trading

As an example, businesses wanting to build new factories or lease offices must spend time and money:

- finding and assessing potential contractors or property companies
- negotiating a price
- drawing up contracts
- ensuring that the seller does what's agreed.

These are the transaction costs, which are all incurred before the business even pays the actual cost of the factory or lease. Economists often ignore these costs when analysing markets, but they are real, as any business knows. We will come back to them.

Incentives: economic signals that affect people's behaviour

Prices are the main incentive in market economies. They tell us whether a good is relatively scarce or plentiful. If prices are high, we have an incentive to look after the good. And when prices change, consumers and producers respond.

Profits are another incentive. They cause businesses to produce. If they think producing a good is profitable, they will do so. Profits encourage new products and new methods of production.

Wages (the price of labour) are an incentive for workers. They pursue careers in jobs where wages are attractive. Low wages mean businesses can find it hard to retain workers.

Incentives also interest governments. Economists can advise on how prices and profits can be used as incentives to encourage people to do what governments want.

Price incentives: unleaded petrol

These days petrol sold in Europe is unleaded, but it wasn't always so. At one time, petrol contained lead, some of which got into the atmosphere. As evidence emerged during the 1970s and 1980s that lead damaged children's development, a campaign began to remove it from petrol.

The UK government didn't, though, ban lead in petrol immediately. Instead, it created a price incentive. Tax on unleaded petrol was kept below that on leaded. Drivers had an incentive to switch to unleaded petrol, which they did. The campaign for unleaded petrol was one of the most successful public health campaigns ever, and all helped by applying some economics.

Summary

Today introduced you to economics, the subject of choice. The world's scarce resources and humanity's infinite wants force choices upon us. It's a result of the economic problem. So pervasive is this problem that we all know some economics. We learn to survive in the economic system from an early age. We have an intuitive understanding of how it works.

But economists are not interested in describing the economic system, although knowing how it works helps; they aim, instead, to analyse and understand. From there, they can suggest how to organize economic life differently.

Knowing how economists work helps businesspeople by giving a framework for understanding a key part of the business environment – that first E in PESTLE. They can then adjust their strategies to reflect possible changes in the economic environment. Economics also helps businesses with its ideas. The margin, the importance of the consumer in the market economy, the cost–benefit principle, using economic incentives and other principles can all help businesses prosper.

Tomorrow is Monday – the working week begins. We'll get down to business then. Enjoy the rest of your Sunday!

Fact-check (answers at the back)

1. What is opportunity cost?
   a) What you get when you buy a good ❏
   b) The next best alternative when you consume a good ❏
   c) The opportunity a retailer gives you to try a good before buying it ❏
   d) A famous television programme from the 1960s ❏

2. If enough resources were available to satisfy everybody's wants:
   a) Scarcity would be a problem ❏
   b) Economists would talk of infinite wants ❏
   c) There would be no such thing as scarcity ❏
   d) Businesses must decide what to produce ❏

3. Why do economists use economic theory?
   a) To baffle non-economists ❏
   b) To describe the world as it is and suggest how people can make more money ❏
   c) To counter management theories of business ❏
   d) To understand the economy and predict how it reacts to changes ❏

4. Which of the following is *not* part of the business environment?
   a) The political system ❏
   b) The economic system ❏
   c) The sound system ❏
   d) The legal system ❏

5. Which of the following is a normative statement?
   a) Taxes should rise in the next Budget ❏
   b) Income tax is 20 per cent ❏
   c) The rate of VAT will fall next October ❏
   d) The tax on cigarettes is higher in the UK than in France ❏

6. In the market economy, producers:
   a) Aim to maximize profits ❏
   b) Are all owned by the government ❏
   c) Own the factors of production ❏
   d) Buy goods from consumers ❏

7. In economics, what is the reward for the factor of production labour?
   a) The satisfaction of doing a good job ❏
   b) Wages ❏
   c) Rent ❏
   d) Profits minus whatever is paid to all other factors ❏

8. If it costs a business £5,000 to produce 100 pens and £5,040 to produce 101 pens, what is the marginal cost of the 101st pen?
   a) £50 ❏
   b) £5,040 ❏
   c) £40 ❏
   d) Impossible to calculate from the available information ❏

9. Governments use cost–benefit analysis when:
a) They want to stop a new project being built ❏
b) One of its projects has a cost overrun ❏
c) Prices rise more quickly than consumer incomes ❏
d) Deciding whether to pay for new projects ❏

10. Economics is a social science because:
a) Economists like to meet one another regularly ❏
b) Economists apply scientific principles to the study of human behaviour ❏
c) Economists think scientific jargon will impress other people ❏
d) It adopts similar approaches to those who study subjects in the humanities, such as English literature ❏

The wonderful works of the market

Some people don't like Mondays: returning to work after the weekend can be depressing. If that's you, then today you can cheer yourself up reading about one of humanity's greatest inventions – the market.

We introduced the idea yesterday that markets allocate scarce resources through prices that signal scarcity to consumers and producers. Today we'll consider how this works. In doing so, we'll introduce some markets where supply and demand don't set prices. In a monopoly (one producer) or an oligopoly (a few producers), markets deliver different results. Sadly, supply and demand work only in the perfect markets of economists' imaginations. But although imaginary, perfect markets are a powerful idea, as we will see.

If this all seems abstract, then be assured. We'll finish with a business guru, Michael Porter. He's taken economic ideas about the market (in the nicest possible way, of course) and shown how businesses can use them.

High theory plus low application: a perfect recipe for Monday's slice of economics.

> *'With some notable exceptions, businessmen [sic] favour free enterprise in general but are opposed to it when it comes to themselves.'*
>
> Milton Friedman

Markets

Markets exist when buyers (consumers) and sellers (producers or owners) trade goods or services, usually for money. Goods traded can be anything from bananas to diamonds, services anything from an employer recruiting a worker (a labour service) to financial advice.

A market's location doesn't matter. People trade in stores, on the Internet, over the phone, by mail, in their own homes, even in places called 'markets' where temporary stalls with coloured awnings are dismantled at day's end. This isn't the only case of economists defining everyday words differently for their purposes.

Freedom and markets

Economists believe buyers and sellers exchange goods and money voluntarily in markets for mutual benefit. Some think this freedom to buy and sell fits well with democratic freedoms. Others aren't so sure. Freedom to buy depends on income, so for those with low incomes this freedom can seem irrelevant.

Economists often disagree like this. They justify it by saying they agree on what they are arguing about.

Prices

Market prices are usually expressed in money. This makes life easier, as we'll see tomorrow. But for now we'll accept money prices as familiar facts of life.

As mentioned yesterday, prices measure scarcity. Relatively scarce goods, such as diamonds, have high prices; relatively plentiful ones, such as bananas, low prices. With one number, prices identify how much the good cost to produce; how difficult it was to produce; how desirable it is; how scarce it is. They also bring consumers and producers together. Both make decisions based upon them. This is wonderful when you think about it.

Money prices differ, of course, between countries. A packet of coffee beans might cost £2.50 in the UK and €3.25 in France. But even though currencies differ, prices are universal. Wherever you are, you need to know how they work.

Property rights

Property rights are essential to the market game. They entitle businesses and consumers to sole use of their goods and assets, which, if they wish, they can sell. Also, property cannot be confiscated. It must be paid for. These rights are upheld by the law, which can be used to recover property taken illegally.

Without property rights, businesses wouldn't produce goods to sell to consumers. If goods could be taken without payment, businesses couldn't make a profit. And consumers wouldn't buy them, as they would fear that they might be taken so they could not enjoy them.

Bartering

One quick point: prices don't have to be in money. They could be quoted in terms of another good. For example, a seller might offer a packet of coffee beans for two packets of tea. If the buyer accepts, that's the price.

Bartering to exchange goods is familiar to schoolchildren. But before you think it's only for the kids, businesses barter sometimes. They call it countertrade. Find out how it works here: www.londoncountertrade.org/countertradefaq.htm.

Demand

Like most people, economists think consumers buy more if price is lower, an idea we used yesterday. Unlike most people, economists call this the law of demand.

Demand is the quantity of a good that consumers buy at a particular price in a particular time period. If you buy 3 kilos of broccoli every week for £1.25 per kilo, that's your demand at that price. If price fell to £1 per kilo, your demand might rise to 4 kilos per week. You could call this stating the obvious, but economists like to formalize matters. It helps them analyse markets.

We won't use diagrams much in this book, but without any this wouldn't be an economics book. So here's one showing the law of demand.

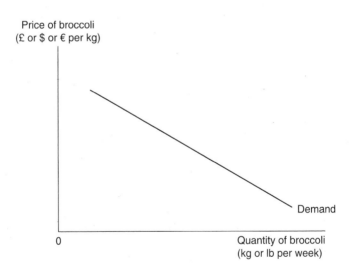

The demand curve

This is straightforward, I hope you'll agree. The demand curve slopes downwards and summarizes market demand for broccoli at different prices. Market demand is the sum of individual consumer demands at each price.

Upward-sloping demand curves

Demand curves illustrate a general rule, but in economics exceptions often make rules. Two types of good have upward-sloping demand curves, which show demand rising as prices rise:

● **Giffen goods** are low-quality, cheap foods like bread and rice that might dominate poor consumers' diets. When price falls, consumers switch to more expensive, better-quality alternatives, because their income goes further.

● **Veblen or 'conspicuous consumption' goods** are those for which a high price is the point. Consumers buy them to display wealth. As price rises, consumers demand more of them: think Rolex watches.

SUNDAY
MONDAY
TUESDAY
WEDNESDAY
THURSDAY
FRIDAY
SATURDAY

What's the price?

A demand curve shows the money price consumers pay. But price includes other costs. Consumers have an opportunity cost for the time spent consuming goods. Typically, it's the earnings they have given up. And they incur transaction costs finding the good, doing the deal, and so on. Adding these to the money price gives the consumer's 'full price'.

Full price explains why convenience foods sell. Buying ready-peeled carrots at £2 for a 500-gram pack when you could buy loose, but unpeeled and unwashed, carrots at 50p per kilo seems to contradict the law of demand. But, when time spent washing and peeling carrots is considered, the ready-peeled version seems cheaper to some consumers. And the law of demand looks just fine.

Businesses can find profitable opportunities discovering consumers' full price. Goods that save time and are easy to access fall into this category. Anyone for McDonald's?

Supply

Producers react to price by producing more of a good when prices rise. They make more profits. And profits motivate producers in the market – or so economists think. The supply curve shows the idea.

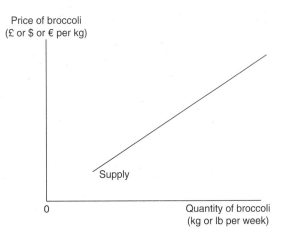

Price of broccoli
(£ or $ or € per kg)

Supply

0   Quantity of broccoli
                     (kg or lb per week)

The supply curve

Revenue, costs and profits

Given that profits determine supply, here's an economist's definition:

Profits = Total revenue − Total costs

Accountants define them similarly.

In both cases, total revenue is the money businesses receive from sales: the price of goods *times* number sold. A business selling 1,000 kilos of broccoli at £1.25 per kilo has revenue of £1,250 (1,000 × 1.25).

For economists, total costs are the sum of the rewards paid to factors of production that produced the goods. These include some profit. Accountants don't do this. They only count all the other costs.

The profit economists count as costs is 'normal' profit: the amount entrepreneurs (the owners of the factor of production enterprise) must receive to remain in an industry. If entrepreneurs don't earn this, they shut down their businesses. Economists think entrepreneurs need only normal profit. Any 'excess', 'abnormal' or 'economic' profit is unnecessary. Not that entrepreneurs dislike this profit: far from it. They like it a lot.

Excess profits mean that consumers pay higher prices than necessary. But they are also an incentive for new firms to enter an industry attracted by the prospect of profits. We will see the significance of this later.

Equilibrium price and quantity

The diagram below brings supply and demand together. It shows there's a price where the quantity consumers demand equals the quantity producers supply. It's the equilibrium price. And the quantity is the equilibrium quantity.

In economics, equilibrium occurs when there's no tendency to change. The idea comes from physics. When scales balance and do not move they are in equilibrium. See how economists like to be scientists!

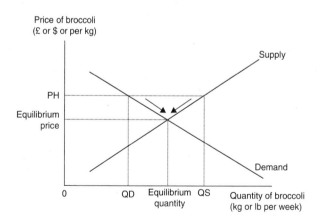

Market equilibrium

If markets work as economists believe, price and quantity reach equilibrium as follows:

Price – PH in the diagram – exceeds equilibrium price
↓
Quantity supplied (QS) at PH exceeds quantity demanded (QD): goods are unsold
↓
Producers reduce prices of unsold goods to attract consumers
↓
Consumers demand more (move down the demand curve)
↓
Producers supply less (move down the supply curve)
↓
When quantity demanded equals quantity supplied (equilibrium quantity), the price stops changing (equilibrium price)

Messing with the market: The CAP and rent controls

Among its shared policies, the EU had in the past a Common Agricultural Policy (CAP). It fixed minimum agricultural prices in member countries, such as beef and wine, to guarantee farmers' income. This encouraged them to produce.

A price fixed above the market equilibrium price, our diagram shows, causes a surplus. But in the CAP, prices won't fall and the surplus continues. Unsold beef mountains and wine lakes result. It's what happens when markets are prevented from working.

Setting maximum rents also affects housing rental markets. If governments set them below the equilibrium level to protect householders, demand exceeds supply. But rents cannot rise. The shortage caused leads to queues and a need for other allocative systems. Again, interfering in the market causes problems.

This makes markets wonderful. Without a government 'tsar' or bureaucrat intervening, surpluses disappear. We want that to happen when there's scarcity because surpluses are wasteful. Adam Smith, who wrote the first recognized economics book in 1776, *The Wealth of Nations*, talked of the 'invisible hand' of the market. You can't see the market guiding producers and consumers, but it does.

Our account also shows why consumers are important. If they're not buying, producers must cut prices. Consumers' central role in the market means economists talk of consumer sovereignty. Markets serve consumers not businesses. The conclusion: in a market economy businesses must put consumers first.

Here's what happens when price is below equilibrium:

Price is below the equilibrium price

↓

Quantity demanded exceeds quantity supplied

↓

Some consumers offer producers higher prices

↓

Higher price means some consumers demand less

↓

Producers supply more

↓

Price stabilizes when quantity demanded and quantity supplied are equal

Again, nobody tells anyone what to do. Consumers' and producers' reactions to price solve the shortage. If you can appreciate the elegance with which market prices co-ordinate the separate decisions of buyers and sellers, you are fast becoming an economist.

If society rejects the market economy for allocating resources, it must address the economic problem differently. Possibilities include queuing, bribery, or planners' decisions in a command economy. Unlike markets, these systems incur administrative and other costs. To paraphrase, the market is the worst possible system for allocating resources apart from all the other forms tried.

The best of all possible worlds

The market deals effectively with surpluses and shortages, but there's another nice surprise. The equilibrium output is Pareto-efficient. Really! This means that nobody can be made better off without somebody being made worse off. So equilibrium output is best for society. Less than it and consumers lose out; more and producers lose out. Vilfredo Pareto, an Italian economist, thought of the idea.

This makes the market remarkable. Individual consumers and producers pursue their own, possibly selfish, interests as they consume and produce goods but the best possible social outcome results. In this view, businesses are socially responsible when they pursue profit! That said, the market system doesn't always work smoothly. Even brilliantly engineered machines are inefficient if set up incorrectly. And so it is with markets.

Perfect markets

For markets to work as they should, these conditions must hold:

1 Consumers and producers are many.
2 Their information is perfect – they know everything about market prices and the goods sold.
3 Neither producers nor consumers can fix prices.
4 All producers sell exactly the same goods, can enter and leave the market at will, and earn only normal profits.

When any of these conditions don't hold, there's market failure. This doesn't mean output is zero – far from it. Instead, market failure sometimes means too much is produced; markets don't deliver the best possible, Pareto-efficient output.

Imperfect competition

Life, of course, is never perfect – you have probably noticed. So perfect markets never exist. That might make them seem irrelevant, fanciful even. But they have a purpose. If they existed, perfect markets would deliver the best outcome for an economy. That makes them a standard to which real markets should aspire. And if markets are imperfect in any way, something can be done to make them more perfect.

In perfect markets as well, you get perfect competition. The two terms are often interchangeable. When markets aren't perfect, competition is – you got it – imperfect. And the best outcome for society no longer results.

Monopoly

A monopoly is a market with one producer, not many, so it's imperfect. As consumers can buy only from the monopolist, it has market power. It can raise price above the perfect market price and make excess profits. The higher price cuts demand and reduces output compared to the perfect market. Output is Pareto-inefficient and not best for society.

Other producers cannot enter the market to undercut the monopolist's higher price and take some of the monopolist's excess profits. There are 'barriers to entry' that protect the monopolist from competition. For example, in industries like water, electricity and gas, setting up a new network would cost a new firm too much. This explains why, in perfect markets, producers should be able to enter or leave the market freely. It keeps things competitive.

Monopoly is at the opposite end of a spectrum of competition to perfect competition. It's the least competitive market structure. Between these extremes are two other market structures: monopolistic competition and oligopoly. The diagram summarizes this:

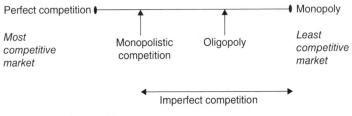

The spectrum of competition

Anti-Monopoly

One economics professor argued that the board game Monopoly® celebrated monopoly when, economics teaches, we shouldn't. In response, he designed his own board game, called Anti-Monopoly, to show why competition was best. This is true: https://en.wikipedia.org/wiki/Anti-Monopoly

Monopolistic competition

In monopolistic competition, many producers (as in perfect competition) sell slightly different goods, which is the imperfection. Brands of tomato ketchup, for example, are similar but some consumers may prefer one producer's brand to others. The producer has some market power and can raise their product's price, as monopolists do. But their market power is incomplete. If their price is too high, consumers will switch to a competitor's product and other producers will also enter the market attracted by higher profits – there's free entry – and undercut them.

You can see where the name comes from. There's some monopoly but also competition. As in monopoly, prices are higher and demand lower than in perfect competition, so output is not Pareto-efficient. But competition ensures producers cannot earn excess profits. They earn only normal profits, as firms do in perfectly competitive markets.

Oligopoly

An oligopoly is a market with 'a few' (three to five) producers, each producing the same good. With two producers, the market is a duopoly.

Price and output in oligopoly are hard to determine. With a few producers, the decision of one affects the others. For example, in the UK's mobile phone market (a good example of an oligopoly), if Vodafone cuts prices, EE might leave theirs unchanged or match Vodafone's cut. We don't know. What happens depends on how EE and, of course, Three and O2, react to Vodafone's decision.

We will return to oligopoly on Thursday to learn more about how businesses behave in this market structure.

The spectrum of competition

Economists use different measures to locate industries on the spectrum of competition. With this information they can decide whether an industry should change to make it more competitive.

A simple measure is the four-firm sales concentration ratio: the percentage of sales made by an industry's four largest firms. The closer the ratio is to zero, the more competitive is an industry, and the nearer it is to perfect or monopolistic competition. A 100 per cent ratio suggests that the industry is an oligopoly, duopoly or monopoly, depending on how many firms make up total market sales.

Other concentration ratios include the four-firm employment and five-firm sales ratios. All measure a market's competitiveness.

Competitive structure and business

An industry's competitive structure is important for businesses. Their strategies – plans businesses use to achieve their stated objectives – depend on it.

The Structure–Conduct–Performance (SCP) paradigm summarizes the relationship. This states that market structure determines how businesses behave (conduct), which, in turn, determines how businesses perform on measures such as profits and output. The diagram shows how this works:

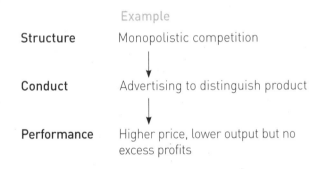

	Example
Structure	Monopolistic competition
Conduct	Advertising to distinguish product
Performance	Higher price, lower output but no excess profits

Businesses must tailor their behaviour to their market structure. It's crucial for survival, a lesson that caused the management theorist Michael Porter to develop a well-known framework for business managers.

Five forces analysis

In his analysis, Porter used economic ideas to suggest that business managers adopt strategies based on 'five forces' that affect profitability. His diagram illustrates these:

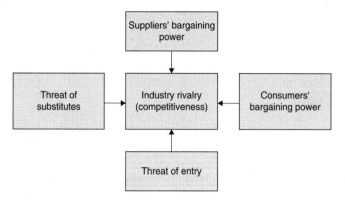

Porter's 'five forces'

Porter differs from economists in taking a business perspective. He argues that managers should identify industries with potentially high profits. According to Porter's five forces, businesses should seek industries where:

1 'industry rivalry' is low
2 threat of entry into the market from other businesses is low
3 substitutes for a business's products are few
4 suppliers operate in competitive markets
5 buyers are many.

The first three represent market imperfections and reflect the idea that monopolies make more profits. The fourth force suggests that businesses are better placed when suppliers must keep their prices down because their markets are competitive – another lesson from economics.

And if buyers are many, businesses won't face powerful buyers (including a monopsonist – a single buyer) able to negotiate lower prices, which reduces profits.

Porter's message is that, to maximize profits, managers must assess market competitiveness. And economic theory gives them the criteria they should consider.

These ideas don't solve strategic problems: managers must still decide using their own judgement. But, as Porter shows, economics gives managers a framework within which to work.

Summary

Today we have looked at the market economy and the forces of supply and demand, which determine prices. We analysed how markets self-correct to remove surpluses or shortages. This is their great virtue. And we saw, with the CAP and rent controls, how intervening in them might cause problems.

We have seen, too, that the ideal of the perfect market doesn't exist. It's a framework. But that's not a weakness. It helps in assessing reality and deciding how to improve it, an essential purpose of economic theory.

If the perfect market's assumptions do not hold, other market structures result. Both the SCP paradigm and Porter's five forces analysis capture why these are important. Businesses must identify their industry's competitive structure and then pursue strategies appropriate to it.

These are important lessons, but there are more – and tomorrow we'll press on and explore some of them.

Fact-check (answers at the back)

1. Which of the following is the economist's definition of a market?
   a) Anywhere fruit and vegetables are sold ❏
   b) The chance the population of a country has to vote in an election ❏
   c) Anywhere consumers and producers trade goods with one another ❏
   d) Anywhere the income of many people is low ❏

2. If a business has property rights over a factory where it manufactures goods, what does this mean?
   a) The business has sole use of the factory under the law and can sell it to whomever it chooses ❏
   b) The business owns only the actual factory building and not the land on which it is built ❏
   c) The government can ask the business to return the factory to public ownership with six months' notice ❏
   d) Consumers who buy the goods can return them any time ❏

3. A consumer buys 40 cigarettes a day when the price of a packet of 20 cigarettes is $6. When price rises to $8, the consumer buys 30 cigarettes a day. We can conclude that cigarettes are:
   a) Giffen goods ❏
   b) Veblen goods ❏
   c) Conspicuous consumption goods ❏
   d) None of the above ❏

4. Suppose a business sells 2,000 products at £1.50 each, which cost the business £4,500 to make. Which of the following statements is correct?
   a) Total revenue is £1.50 ❏
   b) Total revenue is £3,000 ❏
   c) Profit is £1,500 ❏
   d) The business earns abnormal profits ❏

5. When the price of a good is above the market equilibrium price, which of the following will happen in a perfect market?
   a) Price will rise and output will rise ❏
   b) Price will fall and output will rise ❏
   c) Price will fall and output will fall ❏
   d) Price will rise and output will fall ❏

6. What is the CAP?
a) The maximum price in a market ❑
b) An abbreviation for the Common Agricultural Policy ❑
c) Shorthand for 'competition augments prices' ❑
d) An unusual feature of imperfect competition ❑

7. In a perfect market, which of these assumptions does *not* apply?
a) There are many consumers ❑
b) All goods sold are exactly the same ❑
c) Producers are unable to fix the prices at which they sell their goods ❑
d) Consumers have more information than producers ❑

8. For economists, a monopoly is bad for the economy because:
a) It ensures economies of scale if the monopoly is a large producer ❑
b) It sets higher prices than in perfect competition ❑
c) It is a board game that people like to play ❑
d) It ensures a wide choice of goods for consumers ❑

9. According to Michael Porter's five forces analysis, which of the following might profit-maximizing businesses do?
a) Produce in markets where rivalry with other businesses is intense ❑
b) Avoid markets where buyers are few and powerful ❑
c) Seek out monopoly suppliers ❑
d) Look to produce in markets where it is easy for other businesses to enter the industry ❑

10. What does a four-firm sales concentration ratio measure?
a) An industry's ability to produce goods ❑
b) An industry's willingness to sell goods to different consumers ❑
c) An industry's competitiveness ❑
d) An industry's scale and institutional atrophy ❑

TUESDAY

Businesses in the market

Tuesdays can be worse than Mondays. At least on Monday you've just had a weekend. On Tuesday you've just had Monday. But that's no reason to give up on economics. We're making progress and we'll keep it up today, developing ideas we have met already. That will shake off those Tuesday blues.

We have established so far that businesses are part of the market system in which they operate in two markets: goods and factors of production. As we saw yesterday, the strategies they pursue in goods markets should be tailored to the market structure they find in their industry.

Today's discussion develops these ideas by raising a question economists have often considered: why have businesses at all? This might seem theoretical, even fanciful, but, as we'll see, the answer to this question provides practical lessons for businesses.

We'll then look at factor markets and how they work, the different types of business organization, how businesses maximize profits, and whether, in practice, they do. So no time to waste. Off we go!

> *'The main reason why it is profitable to
> establish a firm is that there would seem to be
> a cost of using the price mechanism.'*
>
> R. H. Coase

Contracts

Until now we have assumed that businesses are organizations that satisfy consumer wants by employing factors of production to produce goods they sell for profits. But why have them?

Economists suggest that an economy without them is possible. Single owners of factors of production would negotiate contracts with one another when producing goods. If you think about it, every part of your job could involve contracts. If you needed photocopying done, for example, you would agree a contract with somebody to do it. You wouldn't ask (or tell) them.

You might object, though. It would be ridiculous having market transactions with contracts every time you wanted something done at work or somebody wanted you to do something. And, of course, you would be right. You'd spend more time looking for people to do jobs, choosing somebody, and negotiating and agreeing contracts, than you would working. That's why we have businesses.

Why transaction costs matter

The problem with constantly negotiating contracts is that transaction costs will be too high. Better to have legal entities – call them businesses – with long-term contracts covering work that needs doing. Businesses organize production without the need for market transactions and sometimes that's better if setting up a market is expensive.

These speculations might confirm your worst prejudices about economists. But there's a practical lesson. In any business, external exchanges based on specific legal contracts (market transactions) can replace internal exchanges based on general legal contracts (non-market transactions).

For example, a business currently employing its own cleaners on employment contracts might agree a contract with a cleaning services company. That company now employs the cleaners and provides the service to the business. As a specialist company, that could mean improved quality at lower cost.

If the benefits of an external contract exceed the transaction costs of negotiating and monitoring it, it's worth doing. Thinking in these terms can improve how a business works. And it comes from economic ideas about why businesses exist.

A model of business

Assuming we have businesses – which seems reasonable – economists view them like this:

Businesses: a simple economic model

Businesses take inputs, such as raw materials, machinery and workers obtained in input markets, and convert them into outputs (goods and services) that they sell for profit in output markets.

As we saw yesterday, in output markets, businesses supply goods but, in input markets, they are consumers. And, like all consumers, they buy more when price falls. In the labour market, lower wages (the price of labour) means more demand for labour. Your labour is like bananas. Demand for it responds to price.

Black boxes

Economists' view of businesses attracts criticism for portraying them as boxes into which inputs disappear and from which outputs inexplicably emerge. But the 'black box' problem is unimportant if predictions made using this idea are accurate. And economists contend that they usually are.

The entrepreneur

Economists accept, of course, that things happen inside businesses. They envisage a process in which the entrepreneur:

- owns and runs the business
- organizes the other three factors – land, labour and capital
- receives profit as a reward.

The term 'entrepreneur' suggests a single individual and, in business, individual entrepreneurs are often celebrated. They are creative, innovative, energetic, inspiring: Richard Branson meets Bill Gates via Mark Zuckerberg.

But the prosaic truth in most businesses is that owners and managers share the entrepreneur's economic functions. In economics, the entrepreneur isn't a person. No individual can run a multi-billion-dollar business and, even if they could, they wouldn't. As the entrepreneur's profit is what remains after the other rewards (wages, rent and interest) are paid, unlike other rewards, it isn't guaranteed. Instead, a risky income is best shared among many people and not borne by one person.

When it comes to entrepreneurs, economists are pragmatic and businesspeople fanciful.

Factor markets

Factor markets work in much the same way as goods markets. There's supply, demand, equilibrium price and quantity, and no government or other intervention. Household and business roles are, though, reversed. Businesses buy factors, and households, which own the factors, sell them.

Business demand for factors is 'derived'. Businesses don't want them for their own sake. They derive their demand from the consumer demand for the goods the factors produce. When businesses employ workers, it's not because they like or feel sorry for them, it's because they willl produce goods businesses can sell. So businesses don't create jobs. Consumers do by demanding the goods businesses produce.

The following diagram shows a market for accountants. It's like the broccoli market from yesterday. Only the labels differ.

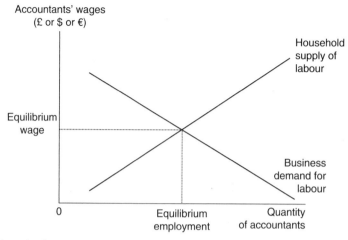

A market for accountants

In this market, businesses buy fewer accountants when wages rise, just as consumers buy less broccoli when prices rise. And accountants supply more labour as wages rise. Higher wages compensate them for lost leisure (remember that trade-off). In equilibrium, the number of accountants employed represents full employment. Any unemployment is the 'natural rate': usually workers moving between jobs. But everyone who wants to work at the equilibrium wage is working. As in goods markets, this all happens spontaneously.

The diagram suggests that to cut unemployment wages should fall. Businesses then employ more labour. Businesses like this idea. Lower wages mean more profits. But, as we will see on Friday, it's not always correct.

Businesses specialize

In all markets, businesses specialize. This division of labour, as it is called, means output rises because:

- specialists in a task gradually get better at it
- specialization increases as tasks are divided up more
- specialists become ever more efficient.

Businesses that produce certain goods get better at producing them, produce more at lower cost, and become more profitable.

But overspecialization has its dangers. If demand falls for its products, a specialist business faces extinction. And workers who lose jobs remain unemployed because they are overspecialized. It is why businesses diversify and produce different products. Rising demand for one offsets falling demand for another.

Footballers and pop stars

The market for these workers is unusual. As you know, they are often paid well. And that's because they are in limited supply. There's only one Taylor Swift. Demand for their unique talents is also very high. Low supply *plus* high demand *equals* extremely high price.

Most of their earnings are 'economic rent': the difference between what they earn and what they would earn in their next best job. This means they would do their jobs for much less pay. But they don't have to because demand is high. If demand falls, though, so do wages, as many fading pop stars discover to their cost.

Money

The division of labour also explains why we use money.

With specialization, nobody produces everything for themselves, so people must exchange goods with others. This could happen, as mentioned yesterday, by bartering but that's inefficient. You must find somebody who has what you want and who also wants what you have: the 'double coincidence of wants' problem. That takes time and effort. It's transaction costs again.

Money solves this problem. You need only find somebody who will pay you money, which you can then spend on what you want. Your buyer also knows that you will accept money, so it's easier for them, too.

Money, money, money

● Anything can be money, provided everyone accepts it. Some things, though, are better. Bits of paper and small pieces of metal (cash!) work well.

● Cash is easy to carry, generally durable, easy to produce in different values, can be made hard to copy, and kept scarce to maintain its value. These are good qualities for money to have.

● Bank accounts are money: people accept payment for goods from them. Cheques aren't money, though. They just tell banks to move money between accounts.

● Bank lending creates money. Borrowers' loans are credited to their bank accounts, which are money!

● Interest rates control banks' ability to create money. Higher rates mean fewer loans (they're dearer) and so less money.

● If converting an asset into money is easy, it's liquid. Hard to convert and it's illiquid.

Only misers want money for its own sake. Most people want it because it's a better 'medium of exchange' than barter for satisfying wants when everybody specializes.

Money has other advantages, too:

- The value of goods is more easily expressed in money.
- Markets work better (which is good!).
- Arranging loans is easier.
- It can be stored until people want to spend it.

Money's a brilliant idea – almost as brilliant as the market.

Costs revisited

In applying the cost–benefit principle when deciding whether to produce, businesses incur costs that can be divided, such that:

Total costs = Fixed costs + Variable costs

Fixed costs such as office rents don't change with output in 'the short run'. This short run is when some costs are fixed; the long run is when they alter. When the office lease runs out, rents change.

Variable costs change with output in the short and long run. Examples include raw material and energy costs. As only these costs change in the short run, it means that the extra or marginal cost of producing another good depends on variable costs alone.

An important lesson for businesses is that fixed costs don't count in short-run decisions. In the long run they do, but most day-to-day business decisions are short run.

Marginal revenue and marginal costs

The benefit to businesses of producing goods is the revenue earned. The revenue from one more good is marginal revenue. It pays businesses to produce as long as marginal revenue exceeds or equals marginal cost. Remember that costs include normal profit, so businesses still benefit when the two are equal. Beyond that, the business stops producing.

As this diagram shows, marginal revenue usually falls and marginal cost rises as output rises:

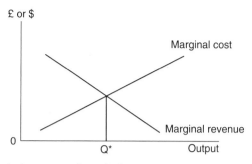

£ or $

Marginal cost

Marginal revenue

0 — Q* — Output

Output, marginal revenue and marginal costs

Economists explain rising marginal costs using the famous (well, to economists) Law of Diminishing (Marginal) Returns. This states: if more variable factors, such as labour, are employed and they are combined with a fixed factor of production, maybe a machine, beyond a certain point each extra unit of labour (normally called a worker) is less productive.

Marginal output falls because extra workers must use the same piece of capital, a computer, say, as those already employed. Taking turns using it means eventually an extra worker's additional output falls. Workers get in each other's way. But wages paid to less productive marginal workers are the same as those paid to other workers. Reduced marginal output but the same wages means marginal costs of output rise.

Marginal revenue falls because businesses sell more only by cutting price. Revenue from an extra unit sold must be lower. It means, by the way, that we are assuming imperfect competition here as businesses set their own prices.

Price and marginal revenue

Charlie's light shop sells ten lamps a week at $20 each. Total revenue = $200. To sell an extra lamp a week, Charlie cuts price to $19. Total revenue is $209 ($19 × 11) and marginal revenue $9 (209–200). Charlie has gained $19 from selling one more lamp but lost $10 from having to sell the other 10 at $1 less. Price exceeds marginal revenue, a general rule for any business setting its own prices.

Maximizing profits

When marginal revenue equals marginal cost, a business is producing an output that maximizes profits.

Q* on the diagram above shows this equilibrium output – it won't change. Below Q*, businesses increase profits by producing more: marginal revenue exceeds marginal cost. Above Q*, marginal cost exceeds marginal revenue, so producing more reduces profits.

This idea often bemuses businesspeople. They complain: 'How are we supposed to know marginal revenue and marginal cost? We never calculate them and our business does fine.'

But the condition is not a guide to running a business. Rather, it expresses the idea that businesses won't do something if costs exceed revenue. Economists doubt that businesses regularly sell goods at $30 that cost $50 to produce, even if they don't know their marginal revenue and marginal cost. Instead, economists believe that businesses behave as if they know them. And, in practice, the profit maximization principle is good at predicting what businesses do.

Business types

Economists often discuss businesses as though they are all the same. They're not. Different legal forms of business organization exist. There are four main types:

1 Sole traders
2 Partnerships
3 Joint stock companies (private and public)
4 Public corporations

Sole traders

These enterprises are:

- owned by one person
- usually small
- able to respond flexibly to customer demands

- good for giving owners strong incentives to work hard – they benefit directly from their own efforts
- most like the entrepreneur of business folklore.

Their big problem is unlimited liability. Owners are fully responsible for the business's debts or liabilities, including having to sell personal assets, such as their house, to repay them. Sole traders can lose everything, not just their livelihoods.

Sole traders also find it difficult to raise money to grow. They are usually restricted to personal assets, bank loans and specialist finance houses. A solution is bringing in partners prepared to finance the business in return for sharing profits.

Partnerships

Partnerships should mean more finance but, in practice, they are unpopular. Partners can disagree on decisions, whereas sole traders make their own. And partnerships still have unlimited liability. If anything, it's worse. A partner is liable for other partners' debts as well as their own. For these reasons, partnerships are mainly found in professions like medicine and law, where professional standards govern relationships between partners.

As with sole traders, partnerships find it difficult to raise funds to grow. They must, instead, consider becoming a joint stock company, as one famous UK partnership, Marks & Spencer, did.

Joint stock companies

Owners of these companies benefit from limited liability. They put at risk only money they invest in the business, not their other personal assets. This makes raising finance easier. It also divides the entrepreneur's role. Owners invest money but may not run the business. Managers run the business but may not invest.

The two types of joint stock company in the UK, as in most countries, are easy to recognize. Private (joint stock) companies have the abbreviation 'Ltd' (limited) after the company name; public (joint stock) companies the abbreviation 'plc', standing for 'public limited company'. In both, an owner's share of the business reflects their investment, for which they receive in return a share of the profits as a 'dividend'.

The two differ in that selling shares in private companies is difficult. All shareholders must approve a sale. This doesn't apply to public joint stock companies. Their shares can be sold freely on the Stock Exchange and this means that public companies find raising finance easier. Their shares are liquid assets that can be sold with certainty, quickly, and at relatively low cost. In contrast, shares in private companies are illiquid assets. Potential investors prefer public company shares to those of private companies. More liquid shares means public companies are usually, although not always, larger than private companies.

Economies of scale

The opportunity that limited liability gives businesses to grow means that they can obtain economies of scale: the bigger the business (scale) the lower the costs (economies). These lower costs occur because:

- buying in bulk from suppliers is cheaper
- selling in bulk to consumers is cheaper
- banks lend at lower interest rates as bigger businesses are less risky
- technical advantages of larger machines and factories with greater capacity reduce costs.

These advantages mean that large businesses (typically plcs) can charge lower prices than small. These opportunities aren't, though, unlimited. As always, businesses can sell only if consumers want to buy their goods.

Integration

Businesses can grow by raising finance to expand an existing business but also by integration. They combine with other businesses in mergers or takeovers. In mergers, two or more businesses agree to combine; in takeovers one business buys up another.

Integration takes three forms:

- horizontal – where a business combines with another in the same industry
- vertical – where a business combines with supplier or customer businesses
- conglomeration – where a business combines with another in a different industry.

Each has pluses and minuses.

Horizontal integration is good for economies of scale as the two or more businesses produce the same product. But the risk is that a monopoly is created that government might then want to investigate.

Vertical integration reduces transaction costs for the businesses. They bring previous market transactions within one organization. However, management of two different types of business can be complex.

Conglomeration helps businesses diversify but co-ordinating businesses in different industries presents particular difficulties.

Small businesses

The advantages of size raise an important question. Why have small businesses? One obvious answer is that every business must start somewhere. Even Microsoft was small once. The market economy also relies on them to develop new products and ideas that meet consumer wants. Large businesses get too set in their ways to do this. And small businesses provide consumers with distinctive goods. Economies of scale lead to uniform goods. Consumers who like to feel different can buy unique products from small businesses.

So big might not always be better. Small can be beautiful.

Public corporations

That said, it was once thought that even joint stock companies could not be large enough for some industries. In these 'natural monopolies', competition can be wasteful and large scale is best. Utilities like gas and electricity are examples. These businesses could be bigger if the government owned them because it could provide more funds than private investors and ensure that they didn't abuse their monopoly.

In the UK, governments created public corporations, such as British Steel and British Rail, that ran entire industries. Unlike other business organizations, they didn't always pursue profit. Governments would ask them to consider social and political objectives.

Many public corporations no longer exist. Since the 1980s they have returned to private ownership in a process of privatization. This was politically controversial, but the economic justification was that competition trumps monopoly. Privatization also stopped political intervention in industries and allowed them to concentrate on business instead.

Arguments around privatization are complex, but most agree that it has worked better in some industries than others. It would be hard now, for example, to imagine a public corporation running a government-owned telecommunications industry. But, in the UK's rail industry, controversy about who should own it continues.

Do businesses maximize profits?

This is another important question. If businesses don't do this, then much of what economists say about them would be wrong. And some economists have suggested that they don't have this aim.

In joint stock companies, for example, managers, who might not own shares, run the business. These managers will not want to maximize profits as owners do. They will want to maximize their salaries and secure their futures by making the business large. And their aims dominate as they are in daily charge. Such businesses will not maximize profits.

This is a 'principal–agent problem'. The company's owners are principals; the managers are agents who supposedly act on the owners' behalf; except they don't. This isn't the only example of the problem. Principals' and agents' aims conflict in other areas. It happens because writing contracts between the two to cover every eventuality is impossible. Agents can exploit gaps in contracts to their advantage.

The knack is to give agents incentives to behave in ways consistent with the principals' interests. It is why business executives are sometimes paid partly in shares. Higher profits push up share prices. Executives then want to maximize profits, as owners do.

The principal–agent problem and the 2008 financial crisis

Before the 2008 crisis, individual traders, as the banks' agents, sought to maximize bonus incomes and make banks too big to fail. For a while this matched the interests of banks' shareholders, the principals, as profits rose. But eventually disaster struck and banks lost huge amounts.

Even so, the banks survived. Governments bailed them out. Traders kept their bonuses and, in many cases, their jobs. It seems that their strategy worked.

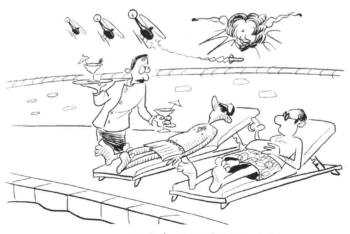

CRISIS, WHAT CRISIS?

Businesses may also not maximize profits because they:

● cannot calculate marginal cost and marginal revenue, so settle for 'satisfactory' profits: they 'satisfice' rather than maximize
● worry that excess profits might cause government to regulate them. They go easy on profit-seeking to ensure a 'quiet life' free of investigation
● have other stakeholders (workers, suppliers, the local community) who, like managers, are not interested in maximizing profits.

The social role of profit maximizing

Questioning whether businesses maximize profits doesn't mean that they won't pursue profitability. Even when it seems they are not, somewhere in the calculation they are probably weighing present losses against future profits. Economic theory about businesses still seems to work, despite reservations about profit maximizing.

The economist Milton Friedman also thought it important that businesses concentrate on making profits. That's how they would be socially responsible. Pursuing other aims, such as environmental concerns, meant acting as if they were the government setting social priorities. But that's undemocratic: their views might not be society's. Instead, Friedman argued, businesspeople should let governments decide social aims and instead fulfil their social role of making profits within the rules of the economic game. Anything else isn't their direct concern.

Summary

Today has been about businesses as organizations that:

● combine factors of production bought in factor markets to produce goods they sell to consumers for maximum profit
● are run by entrepreneurs
● specialize to benefit from the division of labour
● like others in the economy, use money because it's the best medium of exchange when individuals and organizations specialize.

Different types of business organization deliver economic benefits. Sole traders are flexible and produce unique products for consumers. Joint stock companies can exploit economies of scale and sell to consumers at lower prices. But when owners and managers of businesses are no longer the same people, it undermines the idea of businesses maximizing profits by producing where marginal revenue equals marginal cost, an idea that underpins economists' views on how businesses behave. Ultimately, economists rely on their predictions being accurate. And, overall, they are.

But businesses must also satisfy the demands of potential consumers to succeed in markets. So tomorrow we examine economists' views on consumers and how businesses can benefit from knowing about them. It will open your eyes!

Fact-check (answers at the back)

1. Why do economists think businesses exist?
   a) Managers would have nowhere to work if they didn't ❏
   b) The transaction costs of arranging individual contracts among factors of production sometimes exceeds the benefits of producing nothing ❏
   c) The transaction costs of setting up a business are always lower than using market contracts ❏
   d) The transaction costs of setting up a business are sometimes lower than arranging individual contracts among factors of production ❏

2. What is the role of the entrepreneur?
   a) To organize the other factors of production and take on the risks of production ❏
   b) To act as a French translator when dealing with overseas customers ❏
   c) To ensure that the income of the other factors of production is kept to a minimum ❏
   d) To advocate the role of consumers in dealing with governments ❏

3. Why do economists think factor markets are like those for goods?
   a) Single producers dominate both ❏
   b) Businesses are the consumers in both markets ❏
   c) Both operate on the principles of supply and demand ❏
   d) Workers, like goods, are unable to express their opinions ❏

4. Which of the following is *not* an advantage of specialization?
   a) Output is higher when businesses specialize ❏
   b) Workers become more efficient in their tasks ❏
   c) Learning by doing ensures higher standards of production ❏
   d) Goods produced can always be sold ❏

5. Which of these ideas justifies the use of money?
   a) It is less efficient as a medium of exchange than barter ❏
   b) It makes misers happy ❏
   c) It ensures that bankers receive good bonuses ❏
   d) It is more efficient as a medium of exchange than barter ❏

6. According to economists, which of the following ensures that businesses maximize profits?
a) They cannot sell any more goods ❏
b) They produce when their marginal cost of production exceeds the marginal revenue from their sales ❏
c) They produce when the marginal cost of what they produce equals the marginal revenue of their sales ❏
d) Owners let managers set priorities ❏

7. If the price of DVDs rises from $10 to $15 and sales fall from 5 to 4 units per day, what is the marginal revenue?
a) $5 ❏
b) $10 ❏
c) $15 ❏
d) $20 ❏

8. In economics, what is a principal?
a) The head of a college ❏
b) The individual or individuals who employ an agent to act on their behalf ❏
c) The individual or individuals who work for an agent on their behalf ❏
d) An idea, such as comparative advantage, that economists use to help them understand the real world ❏

9. Which is the best definition of unlimited liability?
a) Owners of the business never have to repay their debts ❏
b) Owners of the business only repay debts if the business makes profits ❏
c) Owners of the business will be expected to repay business debts with their personal assets if the business's assets are insufficient ❏
d) Owners of the business always use their personal assets to repay any debts incurred by the business ❏

10. Which of the following explains why a business might *not* try to maximize profits?
a) Owners want a quiet life free of interference from government ❏
b) Only the managers of the business want to maximize profits ❏
c) Marginal revenue must always exceed marginal cost ❏
d) Rising costs reduce profits ❏

WEDNESDAY

Knowing your consumers

It is already the middle of our week; time passes quickly when you're doing economics! But there's no time to relax. Instead, today we will uncover more about economists' views on consumers.

We already know economists define production as satisfying consumer wants. That puts consumers at the heart of the market economy. We've also established that the ability and desire of consumers to buy the goods businesses produce depend on prices. But businesses can do more than just set a price and see what happens in the market, for consumer demand depends on more than just prices.

This means that today we will see how:

- the demand curve helps businesses think about setting prices to increase profits
- 'other things' affect consumer demand – income, prices of other goods and consumer tastes
- economists use elasticity of demand to measure the responses of demand to whatever affects it.

Let's look now at what this involves!

> *'Every fall, however slight, in the price of a commodity in general use, will, other things being equal, increase the total sales of it.'*
>
> Alfred Marshall

The social value of business sales

We know that businesses operating in a market economy must serve consumers. If they don't, rules of the market system dictate that they won't survive. These rules ensure efficient use of resources. It's painful for the individual business that shuts down, but scarcity means that society is not best served if inefficient businesses use resources.

Consumers drive this process. If they like goods, and buy them, society's resources are suitably employed. If they don't like them, it's better that these goods aren't produced. Business sales, therefore, measure the social value of what businesses produce as much as they measure business success. In buying a business's products, consumers vote for them with their money. It would be democratic, if only incomes weren't unequally distributed.

Faced with market disciplines, businesses must embrace the idea that survival depends on meeting consumer demands.

Using the demand curve

On Monday we introduced the demand curve, which suggests that prices are crucial in determining consumer demand. Now we'll see how businesses can use the idea to help them increase profits.

Economists believe that consumers buy goods when utility (see Sunday) or satisfaction exceeds the price. If price exceeds utility, they won't buy. It's the cost-benefit principle applied to consumers.

Here's the demand curve from Monday again, but now with numbers:

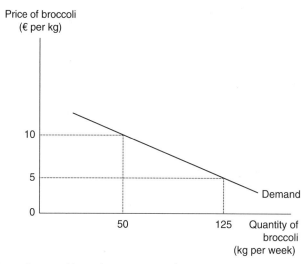

The demand curve with numbers

On our diagram, when price falls from €10 to €5 per kilo, demand rises from 50 to 125 kilos. More consumers have utility greater than price as price falls.

Consumers also have 'diminishing marginal utility'. The more they consume a good, the less utility each extra (marginal) unit gives them. Marginal utility diminishes. Think of cups of tea: the first one is great (if you like tea) but each extra cup is less enjoyable. And eventually you don't want any more. That's diminishing marginal utility. It only applies, though, for a period of time. You might have had enough tea today but tomorrow marginal utility for that first cup is the same as it ever was.

This 'law' explains downward-sloping demand curves. As utility diminishes, consumers will buy more only if price falls to reflect lower utility. Once price stops falling, consumers stop buying.

For businesses, these ideas represent an opportunity. A business with a demand curve like that above could sell 75 extra kilos at €5 per kilo in addition to the 50 already sold at €10 per kilo. If the extra 75 kilos costs less to produce than €375 – the revenue gained – profits rise. But businesses must ensure that the two sets of consumers remain separate. They don't want consumers who previously paid €10 paying €5. If they can do that, then they have benefited from understanding the demand curve.

Utility

Satisfaction consumers obtain from a good is personal. It cannot be measured or compared between consumers. But economists still draw conclusions about utility from consumer behaviour.

Suppose a cup of coffee costs £2. I buy one, you don't. That tells an economist that my utility from the coffee is greater than yours. And my utility is worth more than £2 while yours is worth less. There is quite a lot to uncover about utility, even though it cannot be measured.

Separating consumers

Businesses charging different consumers different prices for the same good are 'price discriminating'. It requires that consumers cannot buy a good cheaply when they would have paid the higher price.

Businesses stop any 'leakage' by separating consumers in three ways: by time, by type of consumer and by geography. Examples of each are plentiful:

- **Time:** train companies charge lower prices after the early-morning rush; bars have 'happy hours' when drinks are cheaper.
- **Consumer type:** children, students, the unemployed, the over-60s can often buy goods at a discount.
- **Geography:** motorway service stations charge more for bars of chocolate than shops in town centres; the same beer costs less in Durham than in London.

Businesses also price-discriminate by:

- charging consumers less per unit if they buy more: 'three for the price of two' supermarket offers are like this. The lower price of extra units compensates consumers for their lower marginal utility.

- selling one-off goods, especially services, at different prices: builders, for example, pitch prices at levels they think different consumers will pay. They estimate consumers' likely utility and charge accordingly.

Price discrimination exploits 'consumer surplus': the utility from consuming a good *minus* the price paid for it. Businesses take some surplus from consumers prepared to pay higher prices. These consumers still buy the good as utility exceeds price, but they don't get as much surplus. Those with lower utility pay a lower price. And this works provided the lower price exceeds a business's marginal costs.

Consumer income

Emphasizing how price affects demand ignores, however, what economists poetically label the 'other things' that affect it: consumer income, prices of other goods, and tastes.

Taking income first, economists think demand for most goods rises as income rises. Such goods are 'normal'; it's what normally happens. But demand for some goods falls as income rises. These are 'inferior' goods. Examples include instant coffee, shoe repairs and margarine. With higher incomes, consumers switch to more expensive alternatives they couldn't afford before.

Businesses should know which type of good they produce. In most economies, incomes rise over time, so businesses producing inferior goods face falling demand for their product in the long term.

All is not lost, though. These businesses could:

- sell more in markets where income is lower, such as another country
- diversify and sell other goods, the demand for which is normal
- refine existing products to make them more attractive to higher-income consumers.

In the UK, instant-coffee manufacturers have introduced products that emphasize how like ground coffee – the presumably better alternative – their product is. This has succeeded in reducing the decline in market share of instant coffee even as ground coffee's popularity has grown.

Prices of other goods

Another 'thing' affecting demand is the price of substitutes and complements.

Substitute goods, such as pasta and rice, are alternatives for each other. If pasta's price increases, demand for rice would rise. Consumers demand more rice as it is now relatively cheaper. Equally, a falling pasta price decreases demand for rice. In both cases, demand for rice depends on the price of pasta, the other good, not its own price.

Similar effects occur when goods are complements and bought together, like fish and chips. If the price of fish rises, demand for it falls. But as chips are eaten with fish, the demand for them falls, too, even though their price remains unchanged. Again, demand for chips depends on the other good's price, not their own.

Substitutes and profits

Knowing which products are substitutes for their own is important for businesses. As Porter's five forces analysis recognizes, they're the competition, so more of them means more competition and lower profits.

Of course, businesses producing unique products are highly profitable. As monopolies they make excess profits. It is no surprise that advertising campaigns often say 'accept no substitutes' when extolling a product's virtues. Advertisers probably all studied economics and want to create a monopoly.

Brand names also confer uniqueness. Coca Cola, Amazon and Chanel are all distinct, and valuable, brands. And all confirm the economic principle that monopolies are more profitable.

Tastes

Tastes cover various influences on demand, among them fashion, social custom and population changes (the demographic environment).

Demand increases if goods become more fashionable or socially desirable, so-called 'bandwagon' goods. 'Positional' goods are in this category, too. They include paintings and other *objets d'art*. Price doesn't cause people to buy them. They buy them because they demonstrate social standing. Equally, if goods become unfashionable or the subject of bad publicity, demand can fall. Either way, prices are not the reason demand changes.

As with other influences on demand, businesses can respond. If tastes alter and demand falls, price could be cut, although consumers might then think the good really is unfashionable. Or they could advertise to modify the product's image. A good previously seen as an older person's product might be made attractive to the young. Guinness succeeded in doing this; HP sauce didn't.

Advertising and creating wants

Some economists criticize advertising for creating consumer wants. It manipulates consumers into buying goods they wouldn't otherwise have bought. This idea challenges the notion that consumers are sovereign and act in their own interests, as economists assume. The debate is beyond this book's scope, but shows again how economic ideas can be contentious.

Other things being equal

To summarize, consumer demand depends on:

- the good's own price
- consumer incomes
- the price of other goods, substitutes and complements
- consumer tastes.

Changes in a good's own price cause a 'change in quantity demanded'; changes in any of the other things listed cause a 'change in demand'. This distinction requires refining something from Monday. Then, we defined the law of demand as 'price affects demand'. We must now add the phrase 'other things being equal'. That is, the quantity demanded depends on price only if the other things that affect demand remain unchanged. Economists use this expression to remind themselves that more than price matters to consumers.

If any of the 'other things' change, so do equilibrium price and output in the market. Increasing demand, for whatever reason, increases price; falling demand cuts it. Producers respond to these changing prices in the market by changing their output. Higher prices raise output; lower prices reduce output. Changing demand alters output – and not vice versa!

Elasticity of demand

These determinants of demand offer businesses a checklist for devising strategies that maintain or increase demand for their products. But it doesn't end there. Economists suggest another useful concept businesses can use: elasticity of demand. We'll take the different types in turn.

Price elasticity of demand

If price changes, the law of demand states, quantity demanded of a good changes. But that doesn't tell us how much demand is likely to change. For that, we need price elasticity of demand. An example shows how it works.

Suppose Luton Town Football Club decide to raise ticket prices for their matches from £20 to £25. Other things being equal(!), the number of tickets sold falls.

If match attendances fall from 7,500 to 6,750, as the law of demand predicts and as you would expect in a textbook example, we can compare the percentage changes in price and quantity demanded. Ticket prices increased 25 per cent; attendances fell 10 per cent. The percentage fall in quantity demanded is lower than the percentage rise in price. Economists say that demand is price-inelastic. You might say that demand hasn't stretched as much as price.

Economists have a formula for this. They divide the percentage change in quantity demanded (–10) by the percentage change in price (+25). The answer here is –0.4. This measures price elasticity of demand.

Price elasticity of demand

Price elasticity of demand equals:

$$\frac{\text{Percentage change in quantity demanded}}{\text{Percentage change in price}}$$

The direction quantity demanded changes nearly always opposes that of the price change, so price elasticity will be negative. But economists occasionally drop the minus sign, even though they shouldn't. It's not the only time economists are sloppy using mathematics.

When price elasticity is less than one, demand is price-inelastic. When it is greater than one, demand is price-elastic. And when it is equal to one, elasticity is unitary. In defining these terms, the minus sign is ignored. If you recall your maths, we are taking absolute values.

Price elasticity's significance

In the example, the ticket revenue Luton Town received before they increased price was £150,000 (£20 x 7,500). After the price rise, it was £168,750 (£25 x 6,750). Although attendance has fallen, revenue has increased.

When demand is price-inelastic and price rises, revenue rises. And so must profits. If demand falls, output is lower, so total costs fall, or, at worst, stay the same. Higher revenue and lower costs mean higher profits. Any business selling a product, for which demand is price-inelastic, will increase profits by increasing price.

When demand is price-elastic, a price increase reduces revenue. Quantity demanded falls proportionately more than price rises. The effect on profits is now uncertain. They rise only if costs fall more than revenue.

In both cases, the opposite occurs when price falls. For businesses producing price-inelastic products, cutting price would reduce profits. For those producing price-elastic products, the effect on profits depends on the relative increases of revenue and costs.

When elasticity is unitary, both price increases and decreases leave revenue unchanged. The two effects on revenue, changing price and quantity demanded, cancel each other out. Profits rise when price rises (if costs fall, as is likely). And they fall when prices fall (if costs rise).

Governments and price elasticity of demand

Governments tax to fund their spending. Among possible taxes are those on goods, such as value added tax (VAT) and tobacco and alcohol duties. When taxing goods, governments apply lessons about price elasticity of demand, because such taxes alter prices. To maximize revenue, governments tax goods that are price-inelastic in demand. It's why they tax alcohol and tobacco products: demand for both is relatively price-inelastic.

What determines price elasticity

Price elasticity of demand depends primarily on the number of substitutes: the more there are, the higher it is (in absolute terms). If consumers have many alternatives when price changes, they switch demand more easily than if alternatives are few.

It implies that price elasticity measures an industry's competitiveness. In perfect competition, the most competitive market, where every business sells the same goods that are perfect substitutes, price elasticity of demand for one firm's good is infinite. In monopoly it's relatively inelastic at any given price. And in monopolistic competition, demand is more elastic than in monopoly (there are substitutes) but less elastic than in perfect competition (substitutes aren't perfect).

Knowing price elasticity of demand is useful for businesses when setting prices. It also helps strategic analysis by informing businesses about their industry's competitiveness.

Price elasticity of supply

It's also possible to calculate how supply responds to changes in price. The formula is similar to that for demand:

$$\frac{\text{Percentage change in quantity supplied}}{\text{Percentage change in price}}$$

If price rose 5 per cent and output rose 10 per cent, elasticity of supply is +2. It will usually be positive as the supply curve slopes upwards. Also, as the value here exceeds one, supply is price-elastic. When less than one, supply is price-inelastic.

If supply is price-elastic, it means that businesses respond quickly to price changes caused by changes in demand, for example rising income. When price-inelastic, supply changes slowly.

Housing has a particularly low price elasticity of supply. It takes time to build new houses if price rises. Markets like housing with low elasticity of supply see bigger initial changes in price because of supply's slow response to demand changing.

Income elasticity of demand

This works much like price elasticity. It involves comparing percentage changes in demand and income.

If, in our example, incomes in Luton rise 10 per cent and demand for Luton Town's tickets rise 5 per cent, then income elasticity of demand is +0.5 (+5/+10).

Income elasticity of demand

Income elasticity of demand equals:

$$\frac{\text{Percentage change in quantity demanded}}{\text{Percentage change in income}}$$

Economists cannot be cavalier about mathematical signs for income elasticity. In our example, both income and demand have risen, so income elasticity is positive. The sign tells us the good is normal. Falling income would cut demand and, as we know, two negatives make a positive. By contrast, a negative sign for this elasticity means the good is inferior. Rising income (+) goes with falling demand (–).

When income elasticity exceeds +1, the good is a 'luxury good'. As income rises and consumers spend increasing proportions of income on it, businesses producing such goods should, other things being equal, have a prosperous future. But in the long term, of course, other things may be far from equal.

Cross-price elasticity of demand

Cross-price elasticity of demand measures how demand responds when prices of other goods change. By now, you will know how this works. If ticket prices at, say, Watford Football Club rise 10 per cent, and attendance at Luton Town rises

4 per cent, cross-price elasticity of demand between Watford's
ticket prices and sales at Luton is +0.4 (+4/+10).

Cross-price elasticity of demand

Cross-price elasticity of demand equals:

$$\frac{\text{Percentage change in demand for good A}}{\text{Percentage change in price of good B}}$$

As with income elasticity, mathematical signs matter. When
cross-price elasticity is positive, as in the example, two goods
are substitutes. Rising price for one causes demand for the
other to rise as consumers switch to the cheaper good. When
two goods are complements, rising price of one causes the
other's demand to fall and cross-price elasticity is negative.

Knowing cross-price elasticity of demand for their products
tells businesses whether other goods in the market are
substitutes or complements. They needn't rely on opinions or
guesswork. Instead, by identifying these, they can then devise
appropriate strategies.

If cross-price elasticity is zero, two goods are independent.
Given local rivalry, this probably applies to tickets for Watford
and Luton Town, although this suggestion needs testing. In
practice, cross-price elasticity of demand between most goods
is at or around zero.

Advertising elasticity of demand

Advertising elasticity of demand measures how demand
responds when businesses change spending on advertising.
We would expect more advertising to increase sales and so this
elasticity to be positive. The higher this elasticity, the more it
pays businesses to advertise.

Advertising elasticity of demand

Advertising elasticity of demand equals:

$$\frac{\text{Percentage change in quantity demanded}}{\text{Percentage change in spending on advertising}}$$

But it also pays businesses to advertise if price elasticity of demand is low. Although higher advertising costs increase a product's price, the higher price means more revenue when demand is price-inelastic. And if the advertising distinguishes the product from its competitors, price elasticity of demand falls further because consumers think substitutes are fewer, so price (and revenue) can rise again.

Using the two elasticities, economists suggest that dividing advertising elasticity of demand by price elasticity of demand will give the percentage of sales revenue businesses should spend on advertising. We won't prove here why this works but it's based on assuming that businesses maximize profits.

To illustrate, if advertising elasticity of demand were +0.4 and price-elasticity of demand –0.8, then advertising spending should be around 50 per cent of sales revenue (we take the negative of the answer to get a positive).

Infinite wants more

We saw on Sunday that economists assume infinite wants. But diminishing marginal utility seems to contradict the idea by suggesting that consumers are eventually satisfied. That isn't so. Consumers always have another good to which they can turn. And when marginal utility for that falls, there's another good, and so on through the infinite variety of goods consumers want. In short, you can't get away from infinite wants.

Summary

Consumers are central to market economies. Their demand determines what businesses produce. It depends on price, income, the price of other goods, and tastes. Each suggests useful approaches for businesses to adopt:

- Price discrimination follows from the demand curve and helps increase profits.
- Businesses producing inferior goods must adapt long-term strategies to rising incomes.
- Competition depends on the number of substitutes and their prices.
- Advertising can influence consumer tastes, make a good appear unique, reduce perceived substitutes and ensure higher profits.

Different elasticities of demand also teach lessons:

- Price elasticity of demand determines how revenue changes when prices change.
- Income elasticity of demand identifies inferior and luxury goods.
- Price and cross-price elasticity inform businesses about competitiveness in their industry.

● Advertising elasticity suggests a rule for how much to spend on advertising.

That's a lot of ideas for one day. But tomorrow brings an even bigger one: markets, for all their virtues, have failings too. Sleep well, though. It might not be as bad as you fear.

Fact-check

1. What do economists mean by consumers being sovereign in the market?
a) Consumers are monarchs of all they survey ❑
b) Consumer decisions determine what businesses produce ❑
c) Consumers must buy the goods that businesses produce ❑
d) Businesses can pay consumers the modern equivalent of one sovereign to encourage them to consume their goods ❑

2. Diminishing marginal utility is the economist's idea that:
a) The more you consume of a good the more you enjoy it ❑
b) The more you consume of a good the same your level of enjoyment ❑
c) The less you consume of a good the less you enjoy it ❑
d) The more you consume of a good the less you enjoy it ❑

3. Which of the following is *not* an example of price discrimination?
a) Drinks in a bar are cheaper between 5 p.m. and 6 p.m. than at other times ❑
b) Students attending a theatre play can buy tickets at a discount ❑
c) A business raises its prices because of an increase in fuel costs ❑
d) A supermarket offers consumers three tins of baked beans for the price of two ❑

4. When consumer incomes rise the demand for margarine falls. Other things being equal, what does this make margarine?
a) An inferior good ❑
b) A luxury good ❑
c) A Veblen good ❑
d) A normal good ❑

5. If bicycle prices increase and demand for cycle helmets falls, this would suggest, other things being equal, that the two goods are:
a) Substitutes ❑
b) Independent ❑
c) Complements ❑
d) Both positional goods ❑

6. Which of the following would be expected to cause the demand for chicken to rise?

a) A report suggesting that consumers could catch bird flu by eating chicken ☐

b) An advertising campaign by beef producers ☐

c) A rise in the price of chicken ☐

d) A rise in the price of lamb ☐

7. The price of a hamburger at Hank's Burger Bar increases from $4 to $5. The quantity demanded falls from 150 per week to 135 per week. What is the price elasticity of demand for Hank's hamburgers?

a) −0.6 ☐

b) greater than 1 ☐

c) −2.5 ☐

d) −0.4 ☐

8. If income elasticity of demand for beer is +0.7, what does this make beer?

a) An inferior good ☐

b) A normal good ☐

c) A luxury good ☐

d) A bandwagon good ☐

9. Big Autos plc calculates that demand for its four-wheel drive vehicles is price-inelastic. Advertising elasticity of demand is +0.8. Based on this information, what proportion of its sales revenue should Big Autos spend on advertising?

a) 50 per cent ☐

b) 80 per cent ☐

c) 20 per cent ☐

d) There is not enough information to answer the question ☐

10. The more substitutes there are for a company's products, then:

a) The more competitive is the industry in which the business operates ☐

b) The lower the price elasticity of demand for the business's products ☐

c) The cross-price elasticity of demand with other products will be negative ☐

d) The greater the profits the business is likely to make ☐

THURSDAY

The limits of the market

It's Thursday. The weekend's nearly upon us and, I don't know about you, but I've got plans. So as we're feeling good about life, it's a good time to share doubts with you about how markets work.

Today's discussion might make you feel as you did when you discovered that your parents don't know everything. It was tough, but part of growing up. So think of today as growing up as an economist.

As we saw on Monday, economists call problems with the market 'market failure'. This doesn't imply that markets don't work at all. They do, and goods are produced. But production is less efficient than when markets are perfect.

Economists have identified various forms of market failure, including imperfect information, public and quasi-public goods, externalities and merit and demerit goods. We will look at these and see what businesses and governments can do to tackle them. Such sombre thoughts make it best just to begin.

Forms of market failure

Market failure occurs when markets don't produce the Pareto-efficient output. We saw the problem on Monday when discussing imperfect competition. These market structures have either a small number of firms in the industry, rather than many, or firms producing different goods, rather than the same. It means they fail to deliver Pareto-efficient outputs as perfect markets would.

But market failure isn't limited to these cases. Instead, it occurs when any of the assumptions of perfect markets are infringed. Today we consider these other infringements.

Business in oligopoly

First, we will look again at oligopoly. Many industries, like banking or mobile phone networks, have a few large dominant firms making oligopoly as a market structure look more realistic than others we have considered.

Economists analyse oligopoly using game theory. This supposes that businesses play a game in which they aim to maximize profits. As in any game, they must gauge how the other players will react. The game results in oligopolists reaching a 'Nash equilibrium': they do their best, given the other players' decisions. The idea comes from John Nash, after whom it is named and for which he received the Nobel Prize in Economics. Russell Crowe played him in the film about his life, *A Beautiful Mind*. Who said economics wasn't glamorous?

In this equilibrium, businesses set lower prices and make less profit than if they had co-operated. This happens because, in deciding pricing strategies and thinking how others will react, each business knows that a high price can be undercut. So they all set a low price. It's a 'prisoners' dilemma'. The name refers to a game in which two prisoners think about whether to confess (the low price or worse option) or not (the high price or better option) and end up confessing, despite that being the worse option.

The game shows that profit-maximizing businesses in oligopoly could make more profit by co-operating. But if co-operating is better than competing, the Nash equilibrium contradicts a central premise in economics: businesses and consumers, pursuing their individual interests in competitive markets, deliver the best outcomes. Nash showed this might not be so.

Problems co-operating

Although Nash suggests co-operation has advantages, a major problem for businesses in real markets is that governments won't allow it. High profits and prices penalize consumers, so governments legislate against and punish co-operation. That said, it can be difficult to show that oligopolies are agreeing on prices. Charging the same price is not enough evidence. Businesses in competitive markets charge the same price, too, so the oligopolists could just be competing. Authorities need other evidence.

Co-operation is difficult for another reason. The cartels businesses form to agree prices are unstable. Each business has an incentive to cheat on the deal. They know that if they cut their price and others don't, their profits increase. The incentive to cut price is constantly present, eventually proves too great a temptation for somebody, and ultimately leads to the cartel unravelling and lower prices – until the businesses try again, once more attracted by higher profits!

The art of price-fixing

When auction houses Sotheby's and Christie's co-operated to fix prices and increase profits in the 1990s, Sotheby's was fined €20 million by European authorities. Christie's avoided a fine because they co-operated with the authorities. Maybe they had learned more game theory.

Imperfect information

Another important market failure occurs when the information known to consumers and producers differs. Economists refer to asymmetric (unequal) information. It can lead to incorrect market prices (and so market quantities).

For example, consumers buying a product might be unsure about what they are getting. Technically complex products, such as cars or computers, are like this. Sellers know more than buyers about the product's true qualities. Used car sellers have this advantage. Buyers can't be sure that the car really only had 'one careful owner'. Businesses also have this problem in labour markets where they are buyers. When employing workers, their information about job applicants is limited. Only the applicants know their true abilities.

But it's not always sellers who know more. Sometimes buyers do. Insurance companies face this problem. Those insuring against risks such as illness know how healthy they are. The company does not. That makes it hard to decide the insurance premium (price) they should charge.

Strategies for asymmetric information

If businesses have more information, advertising their product helps. The message it sends to consumers is that they would not spend large amounts of money advertising if their product could not meet expectations. It reassures consumers about a product of which they might know little.

Businesses also offer warranties. A car company offering a five-year guarantee on its cars says to consumers: 'We're so confident our product is good we can make this generous offer. You know that, if our cars were poor, we'd go out of business meeting the terms of the offer. So they must be good.' Again, consumers are reassured.

In markets where consumers lack information, businesses must develop and protect their reputation. Consumers judge products on this when they have limited information on which to base buying decisions. Anything undermining reputation is potentially disastrous. VW, the German car manufacturer, learned this lesson when, in September 2015, it emerged they had manipulated emissions testing of their vehicles.

These strategies are 'signalling'. Businesses indirectly tell consumers their products are good. But if consumers had perfect information they wouldn't need to be convinced of a product's quality by advertising or warranties. They would know it was good. So resources used on signalling activities are socially wasteful. For economists, signals are 'second-best' solutions. Only markets where information is perfect are 'first-best'.

University: a waste of time?

In labour markets where workers are sellers and information is asymmetric, university education is the signal. Employers think workers with degrees are 'high quality'. Any worker who spent time obtaining a degree must find studying easy and be capable. Anybody who doesn't go to university must be low quality.

In this view, degrees don't improve workers. They simply tell employers about worker quality. University education is, therefore, socially wasteful! If businesses had perfect information about workers it would save the time and expense of university education. But businesses' information is imperfect, so we have universities instead. All of which is, of course, highly controversial. But that's economics for you.

Asymmetric information in insurance markets

Two problems caused by asymmetric information can be explained using insurance markets: adverse selection and moral hazard.

To illustrate adverse selection, suppose a health insurer has two potential types of customer, high-risk and low-risk. It knows that half are in each category but not which category an individual customer falls into. High-risk customers are less healthy and more likely to make claims on their policies; healthier, low-risk consumers make fewer claims.

With perfect information the insurance company would charge high-risk consumers more than low-risk, to reflect the likelihood of claims. Let's say these premiums should be £1,000 and £300 per year respectively. But being unable to identify different customer types, the company doesn't know what to charge a given customer.

One solution is to take the average of the two premiums and set a single premium of £650. At this price, high-risk customers think they are getting a bargain, as they are likely to make claims. But low-risk customers think the insurance is too expensive and won't buy. The insurance company sells only to high-risk consumers paying £650. As the premium should be £1,000 to reflect the nature of their customers, the company makes a loss. This is adverse selection: businesses deal with those who, from their perspective, are less desirable customers.

Moral hazard occurs when a person or persons are protected against the consequences of their actions and so behave differently. For example, if I have insured my house contents, I might become careless about securing the house when going out. Even if I am burgled, I will get the money to replace my contents. The insurance company can't observe or control my behaviour – imperfect information! – so they face potentially huge claims and associated losses.

Banks and moral hazard

After the 2008 financial crisis, many feel that a moral hazard exists with banks. If they behave riskily, they either make large profits, which they keep, or they make large losses and the government bails them out. With that guarantee, which is a form of insurance, they will always behave riskily. In managing the banks, governments face difficulties similar to insurance companies.

Strategies for insurance markets

Insurance companies can, though, adopt strategies to alleviate problems of asymmetric information. If they could not, they would not exist, and we know they do.

One approach is questioning consumers to uncover risk. If you have ever bought insurance, you will know that insurers ask you for certain details: age, where you live, and so on. And if it emerges later that you didn't tell the truth, the insurance policy is invalidated. It's in the small print.

This addresses adverse selection. Using consumer responses, the company can charge different premiums depending on risk. Adverse selection is not entirely avoided. Only complete information on consumers could do that and that's too expensive to collect. But companies do enough to make their business profitable.

To mitigate moral hazard, insurance companies use 'excesses' or 'deductibles' on policies. These require policyholders to pay the first part of any claim. If consumers know they must do this, they are more careful than if they were fully compensated. In economists' terms, the company creates an incentive for the consumer to behave less riskily. 'No claims discounts' do the same. By not claiming on a policy in one year, in the following year consumers pay less. They have an incentive to behave more carefully and not claim.

All these strategies are second-best solutions. The best solution remains having perfect information. But that exists only in economics books.

Public goods

Public goods also cause market failure. Once provided, firms cannot stop consumers using them or make consumers pay. They are 'non-excludable', so consumers can 'free-ride', as economists say: they benefit without paying. Public goods are also 'non-rival': one consumer's use of the good does not stop others using it.

Coastal defences, for example, protect anyone living behind them. Any private business building these defences could not make a profit because most consumers would not pay them. And, without profit, private businesses do not supply. Other examples of public goods with the same problem are policing and national defence.

Unlike public goods, those traded in markets, which we have discussed up to now, are excludable and rival in use. They are private goods. Businesses produce them because doing so is profitable.

Public goods are, of course, socially desirable. The market might not produce them, but people still want them. This is where, as we will see later, governments come in.

Quasi-public goods

Quasi-public goods, like public goods, are non-excludable, but rivalry occurs when using them. Roads are an example. There's clearly rivalry in their use, as anyone who has ever sat in a traffic jam would confirm. But excluding road users is a problem. They can be made to pay, as happens on French motorways, but most roads aren't like this. Motorists don't pay when they use them. In that sense, they're non-excludable.

The reason for this is an old friend, transaction costs. If every road had tolls, the costs of providing them would be huge, as would the value of motorists' time spent queuing at tolls. The transaction costs of a market in roads outweigh any benefits the market could provide. It's better to have non-market provision most of the time.

Externalities

Externalities are costs and benefits that markets ignore. When they occur, market prices no longer contain all information about goods, a property eulogized on Monday. Markets fail.

Negative externalities are costs the market overlooks. A standard example is pollution. It imposes costs on those polluted. But in an unregulated, free market, firms ignore these costs. They are 'external', so firms need not pay them. Those polluted have no property rights to receive compensation for the damage firms inflict.

The market fails because firms produce too many goods that cause pollution. If they had to pay the external costs they impose on the polluted, their costs and so prices would increase and output would be lower as demand fell.

With positive externalities, it works the other way. A good can provide benefits for which consumers don't have to pay. Take health. If you're treated for an infectious disease, you benefit. But so do others. Markets ignore these benefits. Health-care providers cannot charge for them. If they could, they would produce more. But, again, property rights don't exist. This time, market failure means that output is too low. When governments provide health care they think of externalities, not public goods.

Types of good

Using the criteria of excludability and rivalry, economists identify four types of good. The matrix below shows these:

	Excludable	Non-excludable
Rivalry	Private	Quasi-public
Non-rivalry	Club	Public

The only ones not discussed so far are club goods. These are excludable but once inside the 'club' there's non-rivalry. An example is the online streaming service Netflix. Consumers pay a fixed charge to the company to access the service (it's excludable), but then consumers can use as much of the good as they wish at zero price because of non-rivalry. Pricing strategy reflects the good's nature.

Merit goods

Merit goods are those society feels people should consume. Education is an example. Markets might fail to provide enough because some parents won't spend money on their children's education and children might not consume it because they don't appreciate its value.

Merit goods suppose that consumers don't know what's good for them. But economists assume consumers in markets know what they want and buy goods that reflect their wants. Merit goods undermine that idea.

Suggesting somebody else knows better than you what you should consume has dangers. I might think that everybody should buy this book. It would be good for them, even if they don't think so now. I would benefit, but only incidentally, you understand. The lesson is you should examine the motives of those who suggest a good is a merit good. That said, everybody should be made to buy this book. It would clearly be good for them.

Demerit goods make the opposite case. Being thought bad for people, their consumption should be restricted. Again, it's because consumers don't realize what is good for them. Examples include various drugs, cigarettes and (for children) alcohol.

Market failure: a summary

1 Imperfect competition: monopoly, monopolistic competition, oligopoly, monoposony

2 Asymmetric information

3 Public and quasi-public goods

4 Externalities

5 Merit and demerit goods

Responding to market failure

Market failure justifies government intervention in markets. The main methods available for this are for governments to:

- buy goods and services from private producers with tax revenues
- produce goods and services themselves
- regulate producers and consumers in the market
- tax or subsidize consumption and production of goods.

Let's see how they might use these to address the different types of market failure.

Imperfect competition

As Monday's discussion showed, monopolies make excess profits and produce less than firms in perfect markets. Governments could tackle these problems by:

- taxing monopolists' excess profits
- regulating monopolies by, for example, setting maximum prices
- subsidizing monopolies so they produce the same output as perfect markets
- nationalizing monopolies and creating a public corporation.

But governments don't often use these. Instead, they prefer a 'case-by-case' approach. Each monopoly is examined on its merits. This is because monopolies have benefits as well as costs. These benefits include economies of scale, potentially lower prices for consumers, and use of excess profits for researching and developing new products.

In most countries, an independent authority has the task of investigating industries to calculate benefits and costs of any monopoly. Only if costs exceed benefits do they propose remedies. Once again, it's the cost–benefit principle. These bodies also investigate industries where barriers to competition other than monopoly occur. Cartels, for example, have similar effects to monopolies. And proposed mergers between businesses might be investigated because they could lead to a monopoly being created that would not be beneficial.

Windfall taxes

Although governments rarely tax excess profits, it does happen. In 1997 the UK government imposed a 'windfall tax' (a one-off) on privatized utilities such as British Gas and BT.

The economics is that taxing excess profits leaves output unchanged. The tax is a fixed cost, so marginal costs are unaffected. And if marginal costs don't change, neither will profit-maximizing output or price. And that is more or less what happened with the UK's windfall tax.

Asymmetric information

Governments intervene to offset the effects of asymmetric information by regulating markets where consumers are at a disadvantage. These ensure that product standards are maintained. Many products have legal technical specifications that businesses must meet to protect consumers. And if businesses fail to meet these standards, they are penalized.

But, as we saw, businesses can themselves reduce problems of asymmetric information. The government's role is less vital in tackling this form of market failure.

Public and quasi-public goods

For these goods, governments are crucial. Without government, goods like defence and police are not produced, and that's undesirable. Economists often disagree but usually not on the need for governments to provide such goods.

Governments oblige people to pay for them through taxes. But governments don't have to produce them.

Private businesses can do this and many do. For example, governments pay for roads but private contractors build them. Governments act as consumers on behalf of the population.

Externalities

Where negative externalities occur, as with pollution, governments can regulate against them. This compensates for missing property rights. Nowadays such regulations exist in most countries. For example, businesses must control pollutants emitted into the atmosphere. The idea is that regulations increase business costs, push up prices and ensure lower output. Business are said to 'internalize' the externality. With properly drafted regulations, output should be Pareto-efficient, although economists question whether governments are clever enough to get this right.

A policy that economists particularly like is taxing businesses that pollute. Each unit of output is taxed to match the external cost it imposes. The tax ensures that businesses take account of external costs. As with regulations, output falls to the Pareto-efficient level, provided (certainly no small proviso) the tax is set correctly.

Similarly, governments can subsidize businesses that generate external benefits. By cutting business costs, businesses find it profitable to produce more.

The 'polluter pays principle'

Governments could subsidize businesses that pollute. It might help them invest in new, less dirty machinery or better ways of treating pollutants. In general, though, governments dislike this idea. It seems to reward businesses for bad behaviour. So most adopt the 'polluter pays principle'. Pollution should not pay. Taxing and regulating polluters is fine. Subsidies are for the angels.

Summary

Today we have looked at how markets might fail to produce a Pareto-efficient output. Different market failures affect businesses differently and also bring about government policies designed to correct them.

Some economists remain sceptical of governments' ability to tackle market failure. They talk of government failure. How, they ask, can governments know the Pareto-efficient output? And politicians are subject to pressures to intervene in markets unrelated to possible failures. Instead, market failure provides cover for politically motivated interventions.

The policies we considered assume governments know what they are doing, but they could make mistakes. That said, where market failures persist, economists support a role for government in individual markets.

Today's focus on government intervention is also a good introduction to tomorrow.

Apart from intervening in markets for the microeconomic reasons we have considered above, governments may intervene for macroeconomic reasons – those concerned with the whole economy. Tomorrow we will look at why and how they do this. It'll be a great way to start the weekend!

Fact-check (answers at the back)

1. When markets fail:
   a) Nothing gets produced ❑
   b) The amount produced is Pareto-inefficient ❑
   c) Economists become distressed ❑
   d) The amount produced is Pareto-efficient ❑

2. A Nash equilibrium occurs when:
   a) A business is doing its best, given what its competitors are doing ❑
   b) Russell Crowe stars in a film ❑
   c) Businesses maximize their profits in all circumstances ❑
   d) A business is doing its best, given what its customers are doing ❑

3. A consumer buying a car asks a motoring organization to inspect the car before buying it. What does this suggest?
   a) Information in the market is perfect ❑
   b) Information in the market is not asymmetric ❑
   c) Information in the market is asymmetric ❑
   d) Consumers are sovereign ❑

4. In a market where businesses know more than consumers, which of these would be a sensible strategy for them to pursue?
   a) Ensure they exploit consumers' lack of knowledge ❑
   b) Make jokes about how little consumers know ❑
   c) Offer lifetime guarantees on their products to consumers ❑
   d) Cut advertising budgets and reduce the number of sales staff ❑

5. Signalling by workers in labour markets means:
   a) University education should be abolished ❑
   b) Employers have full information about potential employees ❑
   c) Workers use semaphore instead of modern methods of communication ❑
   d) Workers inform businesses indirectly about their quality ❑

6. Moral hazard in insurance markets causes consumers to:
a) Behave less carefully than they would if insurance companies had perfect information about them ❏
b) Behave just as they would if insurance companies had perfect information about them ❏
c) Behave more carefully than they would if insurance companies had perfect information about them ❏
d) None of the above ❏

7. Why is national defence an example of a public good?
a) It is non-excludable but there is rivalry among consumers ❏
b) Being in the armed forces is a dangerous occupation ❏
c) It is non-excludable and there is no rivalry among consumers ❏
d) Generals have more access to politicians than businesses ❏

8. Why are roads not public goods?
a) They are never congested ❏
b) Tolls are a cheap and easy way to collect money ❏
c) Governments do not provide them ❏
d) There is rivalry in their use ❏

9. Which of the following is *not* a negative externality?
a) Air pollution ❏
b) Painting the outside of a house to improve its appearance ❏
c) Chewing gum dropped on the pavement ❏
d) Noise made by workers constructing a major flood defence system ❏

10. Which of these effects would a one-off tax of a fixed amount of money have on the excess profits of a monopoly?
a) Output would stay the same and price would rise ❏
b) Output and price would stay the same ❏
c) Output and price would rise ❏
d) Output would fall and price would stay the same ❏

FRIDAY

Business strategies and government macroeconomic policy

On Sunday we saw that governments provide laws to ensure that everybody follows market rules. And yesterday we discussed how governments intervene in markets to correct market failures. Both are microeconomic reasons for government intervention.

Today we are going to examine how governments intervene for macroeconomic reasons – those concerned with the whole economy. The reasons for this intervention come from macroeconomic theory, which shows how and why they go about intervening. Agreement is not always universal on what to do, but economists, and politicians, generally agree the objectives for the whole economy to be:

- full employment of labour
- stable prices (no or low inflation)
- steady economic growth
- balance of payments equilibrium
- an appropriate income and wealth distribution.

As well as theory, we will consider policies to achieve these objectives (apart from the balance of payments problem, considered tomorrow). We will also refer to events in the economy following the 2008 financial crisis. They revealed much about how governments influence economies.

Lots to look forward to, then, as our economics goes large!

> *'The modern economic system fails to provide employment continuously for all who desire to work. This is generally recognized as one of the major defects of the system, and remedies for the defect are constantly being propounded.'*
>
> Joan Robinson

The business cycle

Economists suggest that over time output in economies follows a pattern called the business cycle. It looks like this:

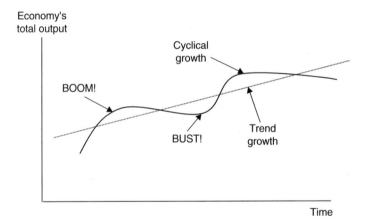

The business cycle

Output doesn't follow the steady course of the line labelled 'trend growth' in the diagram. It seesaws around it along the line labelled 'cyclical growth'. Output increases over time, but it's not a smooth ride. When the economy booms, output grows, incomes of businesses and workers rise, prosperity reigns. In busts, output grows slowly or falls in a recession. Bad times bring lower sales, lower incomes and rising unemployment.

Recessions

A recession occurs when an economy's output falls for two consecutive quarters of a year. The definition is arbitrary but it provides an agreed standard.

Businesses and the business cycle

Booms are usually considered good for businesses. Profits rise, businesses expand, and prospects of higher profits cause businesses to invest more. But booms can cause problems. Rising demand increases wages and raw material prices. Exporting becomes harder for businesses as higher prices cut overseas demand. In economics, every silver lining has its cloud.

During busts, profits fall, businesses fail and jobs disappear. The economist Joseph Schumpeter thought these effects benefit the economy. If inefficient businesses shut down, it releases resources for efficient businesses when the next boom comes. He called it 'creative destruction'. He saw a silver lining.

And busts have other benefits. Prices and costs fall as demand falls, opportunities occur to capture sales of failed competitors, and, looking ahead, good times will return.

Managing the business cycle

Although optimism in a recession is not easy, the business cycle suggests that, if a business survives the downturn (as most do), good times return. Businesses should prepare for the inevitable recovery. That said, businesses, workers, consumers and governments would find life easier if the economy grew steadily. Not knowing when to expect booms or busts makes planning harder. With steady growth, people know where they stand.

Recognizing this, the economist John Maynard Keynes proposed that governments could use macroeconomic policy to 'damp down' the business cycle. Output still varies, but much less, and that helps everybody.

FRIDAY

A Minsky moment

By the early 2000s many economists thought the business cycle was tamed. Hyman Minsky, an American economist, writing in 1992, disagreed. He thought economic crises remained likely. During booms, he argued, people become confident and borrow to buy assets such as property. But these assets eventually lose value as returns on them fall. Reduced wealth means demand falls drastically. The economic crisis follows. This is a 'Minsky moment'. Many think the events of 2008 were such a moment.

A macroeconomic model of the economy

To understand how macroeconomic policy works in a 'countercyclical' manner, as economists say, we need our model of the economy from Sunday. That showed income circulating between firms and households. We will also add to it two other sectors, the government and overseas markets.

How the model works

As the model is circular, we can take point 1 in the diagram below as an arbitrary starting point. From here, money flows from:

1 households to firms as households buy goods
2 firms to households as firms employ factors of production with their revenue
3 government to firms as governments buy goods and services
4 overseas buyers to firms as they buy exports
5 firms to other firms as they buy each other's goods such as machinery.

These flows represent an economy's output: the money value of goods and services produced in a year.

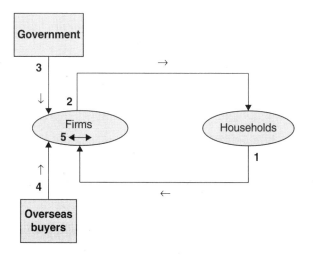

The macroeconomic environment: money flows

The model shows that output comprises:

- consumption goods, e.g. clothing or foodstuffs that households buy
- investment goods, e.g. new machinery that businesses buy from other businesses
- goods and services that governments produce, e.g. education, health care
- goods and services produced and exported to other countries.

The sum of these is the country's Gross Domestic Product (GDP).

The flows remain at the same level as long as nothing changes. That is, the economy is in equilibrium at the given spending or income. Recall from Sunday that one person's spending is another's income, so the two are equal. There is also a level of spending in the economy's circular flow that delivers full employment. Not that the economy must be at this level. It can be in equilibrium below it and unemployment results.

Investment in economics

Economists use the word 'investment' differently from most people. In economics, it means firms buying 'capital' that produces future output; so building a new factory, buying an office computer, opening a new branch are all examples of investment. Putting money in a bank or building society is not. In economics, these are savings.

Measuring the economy

Given its importance, governments measure GDP, the economy's size, to identify economic growth – the annual percentage change in an economy's output – and the economy's output per head or productivity: GDP divided by the workforce.

GDP figures allow for price rises. If GDP in money terms rises only because prices rise, 'real' output has not increased. Economists use 'real' GDP, which removes the effect of price rises. 'Nominal' (money) GDP is measured in today's prices.

Gross national income (GNI) also measures the economy's size. It equals:

- GDP
- *plus* income a country's residents send home from abroad
- *minus* money residents send abroad.

GNI identifies a country's standard of living or economic well-being better than GDP. It is what the country's population has available to spend.

Neither GDP nor GNI are perfect measures of an economy's size, even though statisticians constantly try to improve them. They overlook negative effects of growth such as pollution; jobs people do for themselves that make them better off, like home decorating; and unrecorded illegal activities. But they are the best we have.

Real and money values

Money value is denominated in currency; real value is what you can buy with the currency today.

A house bought in 1982 for £30,000, now valued at £180,000, is worth six times more today in money or nominal terms. But if prices are five times higher than in 1982, the 1982 price must be adjusted upwards to reflect today's prices. That makes it £150,000. In real terms it is worth only 20 per cent more.

Macroeconomic objectives

Governments control the business cycle by pursuing five objectives:

1 Full employment (low unemployment)
2 Price stability (low inflation)
3 Economic growth (rising real GDP)
4 Balance of payments equilibrium (the country's exports equal its imports)
5 An appropriate income and wealth distribution.

Each objective makes sense in its own right:

1 Unemployed labour is wasteful when there is scarcity.
2 Price changes cause uncertainty.
3 Increasing output addresses scarcity.

4 Countries must, over time, sell abroad to finance purchases from abroad.
5 Too little inequality harms efficiency but too much creates social tensions and undermines economic co-operation.

Economists mostly agree on these objectives. They argue about which is most important and how to achieve them, but not their desirability. Views on growth do differ, however: some think it has effects, like pollution, that make people worse rather than better off; others think growth helps solve problems like pollution. It's an important debate, but unfortunately there is no space for it here.

Inflation

Inflation is the percentage increase in a price index like the Consumer Price Index (CPI) that measures the economy's average price level. But beware: a rise in one good's price is not inflation. Prices regularly change in market economies as goods become scarcer or less scarce. As we have seen, that's how markets work. A higher price for a good therefore is not necessarily inflation. It could just be that the good is scarcer.

Macroeconomic policies

Economists suggest three types of macroeconomic policy to achieve the macroeconomic objectives:

1 **Fiscal policy**: changing government spending and taxes
2 **Monetary policy**: changing interest rates and the money supply
3 **Direct controls**: changing regulations and other rules to cut business costs.

Fiscal and monetary policy can alter aggregate demand: the total demand (or spending) in the economy. This demand, like GDP, comprises:

● consumer spending (or household spending)
● investment spending by businesses (or firms)
● government spending on goods and services
● export spending by overseas consumers.

Aggregate demand and unemployment

If aggregate demand is low (or weak):

- less money flows to firms in the circular flow
- firms cut output and lay off workers
- unemployment rises
- the economy goes into recession.

To offset such effects, governments can raise aggregate demand in the circular flow by borrowing to spend more themselves. They don't increase taxes to pay for the spending. That would cancel out its effects by withdrawing money from the circular flow. This is 'expansionary' fiscal policy aimed at cutting unemployment.

Fiscal policy in the 2008 financial crisis

When the global financial crisis hit in 2008, firms' and households' demand collapsed in Western economies. Exports fell, too, as all economies faced similar problems. The crisis was global. Falling demand among households, firms, and overseas customers caused aggregate demand and output to fall. Unemployment rose rapidly.

To tackle these problems, governments around the world increased spending and borrowing in 2009. In 2010 output recovered in most economies.

Reducing taxes also increases aggregate demand. Lower income tax encourages households to spend more and lower profit taxes encourage businesses to invest.

In booms, governments can cut spending or raise taxes. Fiscal policy is then contractionary.

Keynes proposed these ideas in the 1930s to cure high unemployment at the time. But they contradict an idea we met on Tuesday – that reducing wages cuts unemployment. In Keynes's view, lower wages reduce household incomes, aggregate demand falls, and unemployment rises.

Economists therefore distinguish 'demand-deficient unemployment' caused by low demand from 'real-wage

FRIDAY

unemployment' that high wages cause. When tackling unemployment, a government must know which type it is dealing with.

Technology and unemployment

Labour-saving technology can cost workers their jobs. But it doesn't mean technology causes unemployment. That's the 'lump of labour fallacy', which supposes that work to be done in an economy is fixed. But if wants are infinite, the work to be done satisfying them must also be infinite. So those losing jobs because of new technology should find work elsewhere in the economy. If they don't, technology isn't the reason: it's the failure to tackle causes such as low demand or high wages.

Unemployment and inflation

Tackling unemployment can, though, trigger inflation in the economy when demand rises. As so often in economics, a benefit, lower unemployment, must be weighed against a cost, higher inflation.

The problem with inflation is that it:

- creates uncertainty for businesses and households – they invest and consume less
- reduces money's value, which undermines money's function in exchange
- imposes business costs, such as rewriting contracts at new prices
- means accounting profits based on historical costs are overestimated so businesses pay higher taxes
- selling overseas becomes harder.

And if that's not enough, inflation is self-perpetuating because of people's expectations about it.

Expected inflation

Expected inflation is what people in the economy think inflation will be. It is important because they base their decisions on it.

If workers expect inflation to be 2 per cent, for example, they will want their wages to increase that much. Offered a 1 per cent increase, they think that they will be worse off. The same goes for businesses deciding price increases. They will include in their decisions what they think wage increases will be. And that depends on expected inflation. So they increase prices accordingly. Inflation becomes embedded in the economy at the expected rate and feeds on itself.

Causes of inflation

Economists think there are two main causes:

- demand inflation due to higher aggregate demand
- expected inflation due to what people think.

They are related. To cut expected inflation, governments must cut demand. This reduces inflation and expected inflation falls. But lower demand brings higher unemployment as a cost.

Controlling inflationary expectations is as important as controlling aggregate demand. Government ministers often declare that inflation is under control. They are reassuring people that inflation will not rise because, if people think it will rise, then it will!

Fiscal policy and unemployment: a problem

If governments increase aggregate demand to cut unemployment, the resulting higher inflation eventually causes unemployment to rise again. This happens because the workers who took the new jobs when demand rose thought expected inflation was lower. When they find actual inflation has risen, they feel worse off and leave their jobs. Remember that labour's supply curve shows that some workers work only for higher wages. They are the ones who quit.

This effect has caused some economists to argue that fiscal policy cannot cut unemployment. It only increases the economy's long-term inflation rate. Different policies are needed for controlling unemployment, based on the factor market model we considered on Tuesday rather than macroeconomic models. If governments increase demand, they simply increase inflation. It is best to leave the market to achieve full employment, or the 'natural rate' of unemployment, and not interfere with it.

The dispute about how best to reduce unemployment continues among macroeconomists.

Monetary policy and aggregate demand

Monetary policy, controlling interest rates and the money supply, also affects aggregate demand. Higher interest rates, for example, make borrowing more expensive. Households borrow less to consume and firms less to invest. Aggregate demand falls. Changes in the supply of money in the economy do the same. If the money supply falls, interest rates rise. Interest rates are the price of money, so making it scarcer increases its price. It is supply and demand again.

In many countries, the central bank conducts monetary policy. The UK's central bank, the Bank of England, is independent of the government to ensure that political reasons do not influence interest rates. But it has a target inflation rate set by the government that it must achieve. For more on the Bank, see: http://www.bankofengland.co.uk/Pages/home.aspx

An independent central bank also helps to control expected inflation. If a central banker says inflation will remain at 2 per cent, people usually believe them. When a politician says it, people can be sceptical.

Monetary policy in the 2008 financial crisis

In the 2008 financial crisis, central banks cut interest rates to reverse falling demand. In the UK they reached 0.5 per cent and in the USA and Europe 0.25 per cent. But at rates this low a 'liquidity trap' occurs. Central banks cannot cut interest rates any more, so people simply hold money and don't spend it. Monetary policy has no effect.

To counter this, in 2009 and 2010 central banks in the USA and UK started using 'quantitative easing', sometimes called 'printing money'. The European Central Bank adopted the policy in 2015. It involves central banks buying financial assets from banks and businesses in return for money from the central bank that previously didn't exist. In that sense, money has been printed. With more money, banks lend more and businesses invest more, so aggregate demand rises – or so the theory goes. As yet, it's unclear whether the policy worked.

Aggregate supply

Rather like supply and demand in markets for single goods, aggregate supply goes with aggregate demand in the national economy. Aggregate supply is the total amount firms in the national economy can produce given the economy's institutions. These institutions include regulations governing business activity, the educational system's ability to provide suitably skilled labour, and how labour markets are organized. They affect business costs and the prices businesses charge consumers.

Governments can use direct controls to influence such institutions. They could, for example, ease business regulations, such as health and safety legislation. Lower business costs mean lower prices, businesses produce more, unemployment and inflation fall, and businesses can export more.

These supply-side policies, as they are known, can cause problems, though. Easing health and safety rules might increase accidents. In adopting these policies, governments must apply cost-benefit principles to any proposed changes.

Deregulation

Deregulation is the removal of business regulation. It was famously applied to the banking system by governments around the world in the 1980s and 1990s. Unfortunately, it caused banks to begin making riskier, but highly profitable, loans and speculating in financial products themselves, sometimes with clients' money.

For a while this worked and banks and bankers grew rich. But in 2008 banks ran into difficulties when borrowers couldn't repay – their Minsky moment. While it is possible to point to other failures, the decision to deregulate banking is considered a major cause of the 2008 crisis. It diverted banks from their core activity of channelling funds between savers and borrowers to risky lending and financial products that, it later emerged, even they didn't understand.

Entrepreneurs in macroeconomics

Entrepreneurs are important in macroeconomics for the microeconomic reasons discussed on Tuesday. They decide about investment. Although investment depends on interest rates – the lower these are the better – how entrepreneurs see the future is important, too. If they think a boom is coming, they'll invest. If not, they won't. Keynes referred to entrepreurs' 'animal spirits'. Today we talk of confidence. Anything that improves entrepreneurs' confidence encourages them to invest and boosts aggregate demand.

Austerity

As we have seen, governments used fiscal and monetary policy to tackle the 2008 financial crisis. But the fiscal policy many adopted in 2009 brought higher government borrowing or budget deficits – the difference between a government's annual spending and tax revenue. In 2010 pressure grew to reduce those deficits. The drive to do this became known as austerity.

The economic case for austerity is that budget deficits undermine business and consumer confidence. Both sectors spend less because they are worried about paying higher future taxes to pay off government debts. Logically, if governments cut borrowing, it boosts confidence. Consumer spending and business investment rise. These compensate for government austerity's effect on aggregate demand.

Many economists in 2010 thought this view wrong. Cutting government spending when economies were weak after the crisis would be risky. It would further reduce confidence among households and entrepreneurs. And, anyway, governments' position in the economy is special. They can raise money by taxing their population. People who lend to governments know this and will be prepared to lend even when borrowing is high, so austerity's advocates had exaggerated the need to pay off government debt.

UK austerity

In 2010 a new UK government adopted austerity as its macroeconomic policy. This offered a test of the different views on austerity. Unfortunately, any assessment was made harder because the UK government changed policy after 2012. Borrowing stopped falling and the economy improved. Was this cause and effect? That is a question for economists to argue about in coming years.

Economic growth

Economists suggest that economic growth depends on the quantity and quality of labour and capital, and the technology used, in the economy. Technology's importance is another example of two parts of the business environment overlapping.

Businesses play a key role in generating growth. They invest in machinery and factories and adopt new technology, which boosts labour productivity. And business training improves the quality of labour. But governments are important, too, in:

- providing education
- ensuring a stable social and political environment in which businesses thrive
- supporting property rights that help markets work efficiently
- creating a stable macroeconomic environment that encourages businesses to invest
- setting taxes at rates that encourage enterprise and work
- keeping business and other regulations to a minimum
- supporting new technologies.

Economists also emphasize government's role in ensuring that businesses have access to overseas markets, an issue we will return to tomorrow.

In addition, well-functioning banking and financial systems ensure that businesses can borrow to finance investment, including from overseas financial markets, and that households can sustain their spending. The 2008 financial crisis showed vividly that when banking systems fail economic growth rapidly disappears.

Technology again

New technology might boost growth, but businesses don't always use the best available. Sometimes technology becomes ingrained in the economy and hard to replace even if better alternatives exist. The technology has 'first-mover advantage', a term from game theory.

QWERTY keyboards are supposed to be like this. Layouts allowing faster typing are seemingly available, although some question this. Either way, QWERTY keyboards are everywhere. The costs of replacing them and training users in a new layout would be so high they would outweigh any benefits the new layout might offer.

Income and wealth

Income and wealth are not the same. The terms are sometimes used interchangeably when they shouldn't be. Income is what households earn in an economy from providing factor services to firms in a time period, usually a year. It's GDP. Wealth is the value of people's assets at a specific time. Typically, wealth is more unequally distributed than income. Although different, the two are linked. Income adds to wealth if people save income or use it to buy new assets. And wealth can augment income that falls for a time.

Economics and income distribution

Governments more often seek an appropriate income, rather than wealth, distribution. The problem is that economists do not give clear guidance on what that distribution might be. Instead, they are limited to identifying effects.

Equally distributed incomes:

- reduce incentives to work as people are unwilling to take on more demanding roles when extra financial rewards for doing so are low
- entrepreneurs are unwilling to take risks running a business if they don't gain much.

In contrast, unequally distributed incomes:

- cause industrial and other social unrest that undermines the economy
- create problems when resources, such as health care, are allocated through market rather than non-market mechanisms. Those on low incomes lose out and that might be judged unfair.

Whatever the income distribution, though, markets still deliver Pareto-efficient outputs. Did we say they were wonderful?

FRIDAY

Policies on income distribution

Governments can use income taxes to change the income distribution. These are usually progressive: the higher someone's income, the greater the proportion of income paid as tax. Taxpayers pay higher marginal tax rates as their income rises, the marginal rate being that paid on the last unit of currency earned. If governments believe income is too equally distributed, they can cut marginal income tax rates for high earners; and they can raise rates if they feel income inequality is too great.

Helping the lower-paid also affects the income distribution. Policies available include:

- a legally binding minimum wage
- government support to low-paid workers, such as benefits to help with costs of housing and child care
- benefits to the unemployed, ill, and disabled.

Taxes like VAT that affect the price of goods are regressive. Those on high incomes pay a lower proportion of income in tax than those on low incomes, as the tax paid on a good is fixed in money terms. The balance between such taxes and income tax in an economy has important effects on how incomes are distributed.

Inflation and wealth distribution

Inflation affects wealth distribution by benefiting borrowers and disadvantaging savers. Those with loans repay in money so that, with time, inflation reduces the real value of repayments. The value of savings also remains constant in money terms, so falls in real terms.

Minimum wages

A minimum wage acts like the fixed prices in the CAP we examined on Monday. If it is set above the equilibrium, supply exceeds demand in the labour market and unemployment results. But this supposes perfect labour markets. If the market has only one employer (a monopsonist) that uses its market power to keep wages down, a minimum wage can increase employment. It cuts marginal cost to the monopsonist of previously unemployed workers who would work only at wages above what the employer was offering. The monopsonist then finds it profitable to employ them.

As always, economists must consider real markets before applying a theory and drawing conclusions.

Je suis un rock star

Problems of income and wealth distribution have become more important since the French economist Thomas Piketty published his book *Capital in the Twenty-first Century* in 2014. It was a bestseller and has given Piketty the soubriquet 'rock star economist'. Piketty argued that in market economies, increasingly unequal income and wealth are inevitable unless governments act. But he doesn't think that markets are bad for allocating resources – quite the opposite, in fact. He wants to avoid this important role being subverted by the tendency to increasing inequality.

Summary

Governments are important for the economy. They can create a macroeconomic environment that makes economic life more certain for businesses and households by dampening down the business cycle, keeping unemployment and inflation low, and ensuring conditions that promote economic growth.

The 2008 financial crisis, and policy responses to it, showed how governments can stabilize economies. It also showed how misguided policies can destabilize them. Governments in many countries (and economists, it must be said) failed to spot how deregulating banking systems could spark a crisis that hit the whole economy.

Businesses need to be alert to government macroeconomic policy. Their strategies depend on it. But not only do national governments influence the macroeconomic environment. The international economy also counts. Why this is so, and how it affects businesses, is for tomorrow. A bientôt!

Fact-check (answers at the back)

1. Which of the following is *not* a macroeconomic objective of governments?
   a) A fall in the price level over time ❑
   b) Full employment of labour ❑
   c) A balance of payments equilibrium ❑
   d) A steady, positive rate of economic growth ❑

2. Gross Domestic Product is the sum of:
   a) All the spending in a national economy during a year ❑
   b) Spending by a national government during a year ❑
   c) Those parts of business activity governments find offensive ❑
   d) The output produced by domestic servants during a year ❑

3. A rise in a country's Gross National Income means well-being has increased unless:
   a) Workers take more leisure time ❑
   b) Pollution rises ❑
   c) DIY activity is measured ❑
   d) All incomes are fully declared to tax authorities ❑

4. What does fiscal policy involve?
   a) Using interest rates to control the economy ❑
   b) Paying bankers more than everybody else ❑
   c) Reducing illegal immigration into the country ❑
   d) Using government taxes and spending to control the economy ❑

5. If aggregate demand rises, we would expect:
   a) Employment to fall ❑
   b) Inflation to fall ❑
   c) Unemployment to fall ❑
   d) Nothing to happen in the economy ❑

6. A rise in sales taxes on goods is an example of:
   a) Contractionary fiscal policy ❑
   b) Government doing something to seek re-election ❑
   c) Expansionary fiscal policy ❑
   d) Fiscally neutral policy ❑

7. If interest rates in the economy fell, which of the following would be unlikely to happen?
   a) The price of houses would rise ❑
   b) Bank loans to households would fall ❑
   c) Businesses would invest more ❑
   d) Inflation would rise ❑

8. The inflation rate in an economy can be thought of as:
   a) The average price of all goods in the economy ❑
   b) The sum of demand inflation and expected inflation ❑
   c) The Consumer Price Index ❑
   d) What I think it is ❑

9. Which of these do economists think promote economic growth?
a) An increase in the quality of capital in the economy ❑
b) Reduced spending on education and training ❑
c) Rising house prices ❑
d) A political crisis in a country ❑

10. Increased income inequality benefits an economy because:
a) Thomas Piketty says so ❑
b) It is likely to reduce social tensions ❑
c) It reduces the need for a minimum wage ❑
d) It gives entrepreneurs an incentive to pursue new business ideas ❑

SATURDAY

Surviving the international economy

I hope you enjoyed Friday night and that thoughts of austerity, recession and unemployment didn't spoil it for you. Of course, economists, like other people, don't want these things to happen. And when they do, nobody regrets it more than economists. They know what is at stake.

Failings of economics are, though, as nothing to its insights. And on this, our final day, we will introduce one of the best. It comes with the unpromising title 'principle of comparative advantage', but shows how national economies do best by trading with one another without interference in the international economy. It also confirms why the economy benefits when workers and businesses specialize. When you grasp its significance, you'll understand an important feature of how both the national and international economy work.

And if that were not enough, we will consider how foreign exchange rates affect businesses when they trade internationally.

It's a big agenda for what, sadly, is the final day of your first, but not, I hope last, encounter with business economics.

> *'[T]he idea of free trade takes on special meaning precisely because it is someplace where the ideas of economists clash particularly strongly with popular perceptions.'*
>
> Paul Krugman

The international economy

The international economy is where producers and consumers from different countries trade with one another. Businesses sell exports to customers in other countries, import from other businesses, or do both. Economists think this trade should be 'free'. As in national economies, markets should work unhindered in the international economy.

The principle of comparative advantage shows why this is so. It also justifies the division of labour, which we introduced on Tuesday. Indeed, when considering international trade, economists describe an international division of labour in which different countries specialize in producing different goods depending on their 'comparative advantage'.

Comparative advantage

David Ricardo, the economist who defined this famous principle, illustrated it with an example. We will do the same.

Imagine a world of two countries, Britain and Sweden, and two products, cars and televisions. Each country has identical resources and technology available. If Britain produced only cars, it could produce 200 in a year; if it produced only televisions, it could produce 50. Sweden, though, could produce 500 cars or 250 televisions. Economists say that Sweden has an absolute advantage in both goods. It produces more cars and televisions than Britain with identical resources.

If each country divided resources equally between the two products, and didn't trade with the other, they would produce the following outputs:

	Cars	Televisions
Sweden	250	125
Britain	100	25
World*	350	150

*World output is the sum of the countries' outputs.

From the figures, we also see that, if Britain produces one more television, it produces four fewer cars. You will recognize this as Britain's marginal opportunity cost of televisions (we have come a long way since Sunday!). Sweden's marginal opportunity cost of one television is two cars, which is lower than Britain's. As comparative advantage depends on opportunity cost, Sweden has this advantage. For cars, Britain's marginal opportunity cost is 0.25 televisions while Sweden's is 0.5 televisions. Britain's comparative advantage is in cars.

With free trade, each country specializes according to comparative advantage. Britain produces cars; Sweden produces televisions. Outputs are now as follows:

	Cars	Televisions
Sweden	0	250
Britain	200	0
World	200	250

The world has more televisions than before but fewer cars. But suppose Sweden produces 150 cars to match the previous world car output of 350. Sweden's output of televisions falls to 175. But world television output is still 25 higher than previously.

The world is better off when the two countries specialize. This is why economists like free trade. Higher output alleviates scarcity.

The benefits of trade

Trade is also not a zero-sum game: one country's gain is not another's loss. Everyone can benefit. Economists don't think trade is a competition between countries, like football's World Cup, where only one wins. With trade, everyone wins.

It gets better. Even though Sweden can produce more of both goods, Britain still produces and trades. That's because comparative, not absolute, advantage matters. A country less efficient at producing every single good imaginable can still trade internationally and be better off. Call me an economist, but that's an optimistic conclusion!

This same principle applies to individual workers and businesses. Even if I am hopeless at everything, I can still find work doing the job where I am relatively least hopeless. That's my comparative advantage. It is another reason unemployment isn't inevitable. And businesses less efficient at producing everything can still survive producing goods where their comparative advantage lies.

Free trade

This isn't just theory. It's had practical effects. Since 1945 trade and financial assets flows between countries have increased greatly because of efforts to secure free trade. It's globalization, the new world we live in.

A crucial organization in this process is the World Trade Organization (WTO). Originally called the General Agreement on Tariffs and Trade (GATT) when created in 1947, it aims to remove barriers national governments erect to restrict trade. It exists because economists have shown that free trade pays.

The barriers to trade the WTO targets are:

- tariffs (taxes on imports)
- quotas and voluntary export restraints (limits on import numbers)
- subsidies (exporters receive government aid)
- technical trading rules (governments make it harder for overseas producers to meet standards in their country).

Such policies protect a country's producers from foreign competition. Collectively, they represent protectionism. They are often popular because governments appear to be defending national interests. But, as in domestic markets, economists think interfering in free trade causes inefficiency, keeps consumer prices higher and reduces output.

The EU also promotes free trade. Most trade barriers between its members have been removed. The EU's commitment to free trade is, though, limited. It is a customs union, so free trade applies only between members and not with the rest of the world. A 'Common External Tariff' – every country has the same tariff – applies when members trade certain goods with non-member countries.

Regional trading agreements

The EU is an example of a Regional Trading Agreement (RTA). Others include Mercosur in South America, and ASEAN in South-east Asia.

Like other RTAs, the EU offers businesses:

- no trade barriers, to make selling overseas easier
- the ability to sell goods produced for domestic markets throughout the EU's 'single market'
- a potentially huge market
- the chance to ask the European Court of Justice to enforce EU trading rules if national governments breach them.

Free trade and business

Although economists think free trade serves the national interest, businesses benefiting from protectionism tend to disagree. For them, less overseas competition increases profit. And their workers like protectionism, too. Jobs are protected.

Businesses might even campaign for protectionist policies among sympathetic politicians, although economists think such behaviour wastes resources. It's 'directly unproductive profit-seeking'. Businesses do nothing but increase profits for themselves at consumers' expense. And it can disadvantage other businesses that lose the benefits overseas markets offer:

- Exports use spare capacity that otherwise goes to waste.
- Higher output brings economies of scale.
- Profits are higher if businesses can sell products at a premium in markets where they have rarity value.

- Trading risks are spread: if the home market is in recession overseas markets might not be.
- More efficient suppliers might be found in overseas markets.

Clearly, what is good for one business is not good for all.

Porter and free trade

Michael Porter, the management theorist we met on Monday, also offers ideas to businesses about trade. Again, he uses a diagram to illustrate his thinking:

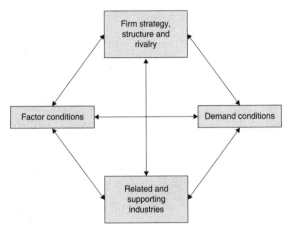

Porter's 'Diamond'

In an approach similar to his five forces analysis, the 'diamond' identifies conditions for domestic markets that make trading overseas profitable and give businesses 'global competitive advantage'. Although pitched in business terms, his model once more relies on economic ideas.

As the diagram shows, to be globally successful businesses need:

- **factor conditions**: access to cheap factors of production; this is comparative advantage
- **demand conditions**: exacting local demand that requires products to meet a high standard
- **firm strategy, structure and rivalry**: a highly competitive local market to ensure efficiency; perfect competition again

- **related and supporting industries**: well-developed links to competitive suppliers to obtain the low costs specialized suppliers offer.

The diagram also shows the different conditions working together. For example, consumers with high standards are more likely when rivalry is intense between businesses in an industry.

According to Porter, governments promote competitive advantage by:

- encouraging businesses to raise standards
- stimulating demand for new, technically advanced products
- providing support for the skills industries require
- ensuring a competitive domestic environment by regulating anti-competitive behaviour.

The German car industry: a case of global competitive advantage*

Determinants of global competitive advantage	Conditions in the German market
Factor conditions	Skilled labour force; engineering tradition; vocational training linking academic programmes with industry's needs
Demand conditions	German consumers demand high quality; few speed limits on autobahns
Firm strategy, structure and rivalry	Several competing high-quality car producers: Volkswagen, Mercedes-Benz, Audi, Opel, Porsche
Related and supporting industries	Highly developed, competitive 'Mittelstand' of small and medium-sized businesses provide parts and machinery to car manufacturers at relatively low cost and high quality.

*German cars accounted for 23 per cent of total world car exports in 2014.

A warning, though: sometimes absence of Porter's conditions creates globally competitive industries. For example, Japan's lack of natural resources caused it to develop industries that didn't require them, such as electronics. The Japanese industry went on to dominate world markets in this sector for many years. And nothing is permanent. At the time of writing, it remains unclear how the VW emissions scandal will affect the German car industry's competitive advantage.

Exchange rates

Given that countries specialize to benefit from trade, money must change hands, as in national economies. But as countries have different currencies, businesses trading abroad must convert them back into their own. The rate this happens at, the foreign exchange rate, is significant. It can cause businesses to lose money.

Economists think they know what determines this rate. As exchange rates are prices of currencies for each other, they depend, like any price, on supply and demand. It's called the foreign exchange market with good reason.

The foreign exchange market

Demand in this market comes from overseas consumers buying goods from another country. For example, suppose overseas consumers want to buy US goods. They will need US dollars to pay US businesses. And if the businesses accept foreign currency, they will want the dollars.

Supply in the dollar market comes from US consumers buying overseas goods. They need foreign currency to pay overseas businesses, which they obtain with their dollars. If foreign businesses accept dollars, they supply them into the market to obtain their own currency.

As in goods markets, higher demand and lower supply raise price. Higher supply and lower demand reduce price. Changes in the international economy then affect exchange rates, as follows:

Increased overseas demand
for US goods

↓

Increased demand for dollars

↓

Dollar's exchange rate rises

Increased US demand for
overseas goods

↓

Increased supply of dollars

↓

Dollar's exchange rate falls

Changes in i) interest rates and ii) inflation also affect exchange rates:

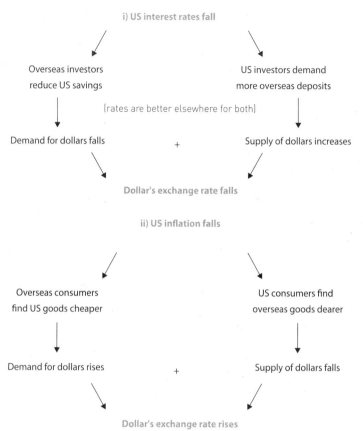

i) US interest rates fall

Overseas investors reduce US savings

US investors demand more overseas deposits

(rates are better elsewhere for both)

Demand for dollars falls   +   Supply of dollars increases

Dollar's exchange rate falls

ii) US inflation falls

Overseas consumers find US goods cheaper

US consumers find overseas goods dearer

Demand for dollars rises   +   Supply of dollars falls

Dollar's exchange rate rises

Similar paths can be plotted for the reverse of these changes. Indeed, anything that changes a currency's supply or demand in foreign exchange markets affects its exchange rate.

Floating and fixed exchange rates

When governments allow supply and demand to operate freely, economists talk of floating exchange rates. But governments can intervene in the market to maintain a fixed exchange rate, rather as they might fix housing rents. The British government might, for example, aim for a rate of £1 = $1.60. They can do this using foreign exchange reserves: foreign currencies usually held by the central bank. The bank buys and sells these in the foreign exchange market to keep the exchange rate stable, like this:

Exchange rate begins to fall

↓

Central bank buys own currency
using foreign currency reserves

↓   ↓

Demand for   Supply of other
currency rises   currencies rises

↘   ↙

Exchange rate rises

Exchange rates and businesses

A yacht produced in Britain costs £250,000. At £1 = $1.70, US customers pay $425,000 (250,000 × 1.70). At £1 = $1.60, a lower exchange rate for the pound and a higher rate for the US dollar, US customers pay $400,000 (250,000 × 1.60).

Lower exchange rates make exporting easier. Here, the dollar price for US customers falls.

If the business buys hulls from Germany and each costs €40,000, at the rate £1 = €1.25, hulls cost the business £32,000 (40,000/1.25). But at £1 = €1.10, hulls cost £36,364 (40,000/1.10).

The advantage of a lower dollar exchange rate is offset. The business must increase the price in pounds to cover higher input costs – or accept lower profits.

Lower exchange rates make selling abroad easier but raise imported raw material and component prices.

A well-known fixed exchange-rate system was that adopted internationally after the Second World War, the 'Bretton Woods' system. The International Monetary Fund (IMF), founded in 1947 along with the WTO, managed it. Countries agreed to fix exchange rates against the US dollar. Rates altered only if the IMF permitted.

Devaluation and depreciation

Devaluation: a currency's value falls in a fixed exchange-rate system. An increased value is a **revaluation**.

Depreciation: a currency's value falls when the exchange rate floats. An increased value is an **appreciation**.

Fixed exchange rates: a reckoning

Pros	Cons
1 Risk and uncertainty for businesses trading overseas are reduced.	1 Governments must hold foreign exchange reserves to support the exchange rate.
2 They encourage trade between countries and its associated benefits.	2 These have an opportunity cost – for example, the hospitals or schools the money could have built.
3 Countries cannot depreciate currencies to gain competitive advantage – 'beggar my neighbour' policies.	3 In practice, foreign-exchange markets are often too big for central banks to influence.

You don't see fixed exchange rates much these days, and the Bretton Woods system collapsed in 1973. This tells you which of these is greater.

Exchange rates and the balance of payments

When exchange rates alter, whether fixed or floating, they affect a country's balance of payments account: the financial summary of a country's dealings with the rest of the world. If annual exports of goods and services exceed imports, the balance of payments 'current account' is in surplus. If imports exceed exports, it is in deficit. And if they are equal, the account is in equilibrium.

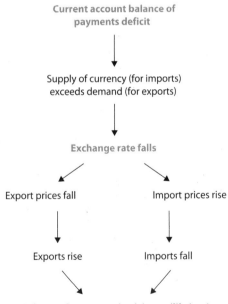

Foreign-exchange risk

A British manufacturer wants to buy tin. The price is quoted in US dollars on the London Metal Exchange. See here: https://www.lme.com/

Suppose tin costs $21,000 per tonne. At the exchange rate £1 = $1.50, the manufacturer pays £14,000 per tonne. At this price buying tin is profitable. But suppose when the business buys its tin £1 = $1.40. The tin now costs £15,000, and buying it is perhaps no longer profitable. That's the foreign-exchange risk that fixed exchange rates help reduce.

When exchange rates float, balance of payments equilibrium should result automatically, as follows:

Current account balance of payments deficit

↓

Supply of currency (for imports) exceeds demand (for exports)

↓

Exchange rate falls

Export prices fall   Import prices rise

↓   ↓

Exports rise   Imports fall

Balance of payments back in equilibrium!

Similar forces remove a surplus. You will know enough to confirm this result.

Current account surpluses are often considered desirable, while deficits imply too many foreign imports, which many assume cannot be good. But this view is simplistic.

Imports satisfy consumer wants that the country's businesses cannot satisfy. Who in Britain, for example, wouldn't want a German BMW? Well, many people, I suppose, but you see the point. Countries must export, not for the sake of it, but to pay for imports they want. And, as we saw yesterday, the government's macroeconomic objective is to balance exports and imports, not to maximize exports and minimize imports. That would make no sense. The country would have plenty of money but many unsatisfied wants. It would be miserly behaviour.

As they are accounts, the complete balance of payments account must always balance. A deficit on the current account, for example, must be paid for. Countries do this by borrowing or using reserves, or both. The borrowing or reserves used then match the deficit on the current account. The accounts balance. And, with a surplus, the country either pays off debts or increases reserves. It is accounting but with economic implications.

Balance of payments equilibrium and fixed exchange rates

With fixed rates, balance of payments equilibrium is not automatic. This is another problem with them. Instead, if governments do not wish to devalue the currency to tackle a deficit, they have two policies available:

1 **Cut aggregate demand.** Lower incomes reduce demand for imports. And firms export more as conditions at home deteriorate. The current account improves, but at a cost: unemployment rises, too.

2 **Introduce protectionist policies on imports, such as tariffs or quotas.** Fewer imports cut the deficit. But such policies are unrealistic nowadays. The WTO would sanction a government using them, as would the EU any member country proposing them.

Business in the foreign exchange market

Given that most exchange rates float these days, businesses trading overseas face exchange-rate risks. But, as ever, markets have responded.

Businesses can buy foreign exchange using forward or futures contracts. These guarantee an exchange rate at a future date. Even if the current exchange rate (spot rate) alters, businesses receive the guaranteed rate. Businesses 'hedge' the foreign exchange risk. It's not cost-free. Businesses pay fees for futures contracts but better that than possible exchange-rate losses.

Futures markets exist for many products besides foreign exchange, including pork bellies, rice, orange juice and oil. The London Metal Exchange and the Chicago Board of Trade are two important markets where these contracts are traded.

Hedging

The airline Ryanair, renowned for rigorously controlling costs, is also known for hedging.

Ryanair pays for jet fuel, its main operating cost, in US dollars but its revenues are in euros and pounds. If the dollar's exchange rate unexpectedly rose against these two currencies, Ryanair's costs would rise. To reduce this risk, the airline buys around 90 per cent of its dollars in the futures market. It also uses forward contracts to guarantee the dollar price on around 90 per cent of its jet fuel purchases. By these means, Ryanair hedges the risk that jet fuel prices, which often fluctuate greatly, will harm profits.

The euro: a fixed exchange rate

When the EU created the euro in 1999, the exchange rate of currencies in countries adopting it – eurozone countries – became permanently fixed against one another. It makes the euro the ultimate fixed exchange-rate system. The idea was to encourage trade between EU members by removing both exchange-rate risks and the transaction costs of converting currencies or buying futures contracts to hedge currency risks. But the euro has demonstrated a major flaw of fixed rates.

When exchange rates float, and a country becomes uncompetitive in overseas markets through, say, higher inflation, its exchange rate falls to restore competitiveness (see above). But in the euro this cannot happen. If Spanish businesses, for example, become internationally uncompetitive, prices in Spain must fall to restore competitiveness. And the Spanish government must reduce aggregate demand to cut prices. But that increases unemployment. And there's the flaw. National economies, like Spain's, now take the strain of adjustment that the exchange rate previously took.

Competitive eurozone countries have, though, prospered because it takes longer for inflation to fall than for a currency to depreciate. So businesses in countries like Germany have retained competitive advantage longer than if exchange rates were floating.

These problems are central to the euro's continuing difficulties.

Summary

Economists think free trade best for the world's economies. But businesses do not always agree. Some benefit from barriers to trade that protect them from competition. For other businesses, though, free trade is an opportunity, not a threat, in a globalized world economy. Porter's model supports this view.

Businesses trading overseas must, however, deal with problems of exchange rates. When rates float, businesses risk losses from exchange-rate movements. Although markets provide possibilities to hedge such risks, there is a cost, which reduces the benefits trade brings.

But as we have seen throughout this week, economics is often like that – balancing arguments to seek solutions. It's what makes it the intriguing subject that I hope you'll explore more in the future, both out of interest and to discover more about how it can help you and your business.

Otherwise, that's it. Our week is over. Let's just hope next week is half as good!

Fact-check (answers at the back)

1. The principle of comparative advantage states:
   a) Countries specialize in those goods in which they have the lowest opportunity cost ❏
   b) Countries specialize in those goods in which they have an absolute advantage ❏
   c) If countries specialize, they risk being unable to feed themselves during wars ❏
   d) Free trade can only be achieved if governments impose import controls ❏

2. Two countries, X and Y, produce oranges and lemons. With the same resources, X can produce 10 oranges or 20 lemons, Y can produce 15 oranges or 45 lemons. Which of the following statements is correct?
   a) X has an absolute advantage in producing both goods ❏
   b) Y has a comparative advantage in lemons ❏
   c) X has a comparative advantage in lemons ❏
   d) Y has a comparative advantage in oranges ❏

3. The following are all advantages businesses can obtain from trading overseas, *except:*
   a) Exporting allows businesses to use spare capacity that would otherwise go to waste ❏
   b) The costs of trading overseas are lower than those of trading in the home market ❏
   c) Trading risks are reduced by selling overseas ❏
   d) The business can gain further economies of scale when it produces for overseas markets ❏

4. Tariffs benefit businesses in a country by:
   a) Reducing overseas competition ❏
   b) Increasing profits ❏
   c) Ensuring more secure sales for the future ❏
   d) All of the above ❏

5. According to Porter's 'Diamond', which of the conditions below would help to give an industry global competitive advantage?
   a) A highly competitive domestic market ❏
   b) Lack of natural resources ❏
   c) Monopoly markets among suppliers ❏
   d) A mining industry able to extract diamonds ❏

6. Demand for a country's currency depends upon:
a) Demand for overseas goods from the country's consumers ☐
b) The central bank's purchase of overseas currencies ☐
c) The IMF's instructions ☐
d) Demand for the country's goods among overseas consumers ☐

7. How does a fall in the pound's exchange rate affect British businesses that trade overseas?
a) Import prices fall in pounds ☐
b) Import prices rise in pounds ☐
c) Export prices rise in pounds ☐
d) It will have no effect ☐

8. One advantage of fixed exchange rates is:
a) Governments do not need to hold reserves of foreign currency ☐
b) The exchange rate adjusts automatically to changes in demand for a country's currency ☐
c) Businesses are not exposed to foreign exchange-rate risks ☐
d) None of the above ☐

9. Which of the following policies will reduce an economy's balance of payments surplus when the exchange rate is floating?
a) A decrease in the country's interest rates ☐
b) A decrease in government spending ☐
c) The introduction of a wealth tax ☐
d) Higher tariffs on imports ☐

10. In economic terms, the European Union is:
a) A single currency ☐
b) A customs union ☐
c) A monopoly ☐
d) A 'Bretton Woods' organization ☐

1 Seven books in seven weeks

- Start with T. Coskeran, *Economics: A Complete Introduction* (Hodder Education, 2012). I discuss in greater detail the economic ideas introduced in this book – and more besides.

- Go on to C. Mulhearn and H. Vane, *Economics for Business*, 3rd edition (Palgrave Macmillan, 2015). The authors do an outstanding job of extending applications of economics to business discussed in this book.

- Then try J. Sloman, K. Hinde and D. Garratt, *Economics for Business*, 6th edition (FT Publishing International, 2013). This is another excellent read that covers key principles of economics applicable to business.

- After that, read D. Orrell and B. van Loon, *Economics: A Graphic Guide* (Icon Books, 2011). Arranged in chronological order, this short text gives you a complete overview of the history of economic thought and how economics developed as a subject to be used in business. It's good for dipping into when you have a spare few moments.

- Then switch to M. Sandel, *What Money Can't Buy* (Penguin, 2013), which examines markets from a philosopher's viewpoint. In doing so, Sandel's highly readable book raises questions about markets for anyone interested in how they work.

- And check out R. Skidelsky, *Keynes: The Return of the Master* (Penguin, 2010), a valuable introduction to the events of the global financial crisis. Skidelsky shows how Keynes's ideas from the 1930s examined on Friday were relevant after 2008 in a world of economic crisis.

- Finally, read M. Jevons, *The Mystery of the Invisible Hand* (Princeton University Press, 2014). This is a murder mystery in which an economics professor – loosely based on Milton

Friedman – uses economic theory to solve a crime. During it, the author – a pseudonym based on Alfred Marshall and William Jevons (a nineteenth-century economist) – introduces economic ideas relevant to businesses.

2 Seven super sites to surf

● The blog of the BBC's economics editor Robert Peston also provides a link to the blog of the BBC business editor Kamal Ahmed who, like Peston, uses economic ideas to analyse business developments.
www.bbc.co.uk/news/correspondents/robertpeston
(entertainment rating 4*; economics rating 4*)

● You could spend all your days following links to economics and business articles compiled by Mark Thoma on this most super of aggregator sites.
http://economistsview.typepad.com
(entertainment rating 3*; economics rating 5*)

● The European Union's statistics website has statistics and discussions of business and economic developments in all 28 of the EU's member states. http://ec.europa.eu/eurostat
(entertainment rating 3*; economics rating 5*)

● The *Financial Times*'s website offers excellent commentaries on economic affairs, often from a business perspective. The sections on markets are fascinating for seeing how real markets compare to economists' theories. You'll need a subscription to access everything the site has to offer. www.ft.com/home/uk (entertainment rating 5*; economics rating 4*)

● For an international perspective, the IMF's website has plenty of data on global economic trends and good discussions of the implications for businesses around the world in the iMFdirect blog. www.imf.org (entertainment rating 3*; economics rating: 5*)

● The website of Nobel prize-winning economist Paul Krugman includes his *New York Times* blog, which provides a feisty commentary on economics applied to real-world problems. www.krugmanonline.com (entertainment rating 5*; economics rating 5*)

- The UK government's statistics department, the Office for National Statistics, provides a treasure mine of economic and business statistics with good commentaries on what the stats mean. www.ons.gov.uk/ons/index.html (entertainment rating 3*; economics rating 5*)

3 Seven quotes to make you think

- 'The theory of economics does not furnish a body of settled conclusions immediately applicable to policy. It is a method rather than a doctrine, an apparatus of the mind, a technique of thinking, which helps its possessor to draw correct conclusions.' J. M. Keynes, Introduction to the Cambridge Economic Handbooks Series, in D. Robertson, *Money* (Cambridge University Press, 1922). As so often, Keynes says it best.

- 'It is not from the benevolence of the butcher, the brewer or the baker that we expect our dinner, but from their regard to their own self-interest.' A. Smith, *The Wealth of Nations*, first published 1776 (Penguin, 1999). Adam Smith was the first to formalize the idea that self-interest drives the 'invisible hand' of the market.

- '[I]f an exchange between two parties is voluntary, it will not take place unless both believe they will benefit from it. Most economic fallacies derive from the neglect of this simple insight, from the tendency to assume that there is a fixed pie, that one party can gain only at the expense of another.' M. Friedman, *Free to Choose* (Secker and Warburg, 1980). Friedman makes a point often overlooked when people criticize economics as a subject that justifies selfish behaviour. More often, in fact, economists are concerned to show how everybody can benefit. If that sounds defensive, it's because it is.

- 'Ask good students how real-world firms set output and price of goods and they will say, "Firms will equate marginal revenue and marginal cost."... Even if the firm is using the most advanced cost-accounting procedures that currently exist and has the latest computer on which to do the calculations, the necessary information for implementing this prescription is too costly to collect.' D. Colander, *The Stories Economists Tell* (McGraw Hill Irwin, 2006). Colander confirms that economic theory does not describe how businesses decide what to produce and what price to charge.

- '(M)anagement has failed if it fails to produce economic results. It has failed if it does not supply goods and services desired by the consumer at a price the consumer is willing to pay. It has failed if it does not improve or at least maintain the wealth-producing capacity of the economic resources entrusted to it.' P. Drucker, *The Practice of Management* (Pan Books, 1979). As a management theorist, Drucker emphasizes the role business managers play in meeting the demands of the market economy. He is right to do so.

- 'The salary of the chief executive of a large corporation is not a market award for achievement. It is frequently in the nature of a warm personal gesture by the individual to himself.' J. K. Galbraith, *Annals of an Abiding Liberal* (Houghton Mifflin, 1979). Galbraith, in typically acerbic fashion, questions the idea that all wages are determined by supply and demand in factor markets for labour, as we supposed on Tuesday.

- 'Countries trade with each other because this enables them to participate in and profit from the international division of labour. Not unlike businesses and individuals, each area specializes in those lines of economic activity to which it happens to be best suited.' V. Leontief, in J. Bhagwati, *International Trade: Selected Readings* (Penguin, 1969). Leontief sums up the situation. In the end, it is comparative advantage that determines in which area of production individuals and organizations specialize.

4 Seven illustrious economists

- **Adam Smith (1723–90)**: In his *Wealth of Nations*, published in 1776, Smith was the first to outline how markets work. His views remain relevant today. He also appears on the back of the UK's £20 note, where he is quoted on the division of labour. It is a fitting tribute to his many contributions to economics.

- **Alfred Marshall (1843–1924)**: Marshall's *Principles of Economics* taught generations of economists. It pulled together many ideas on economics, including that of the margin, which came to prominence only in the late nineteenth century. His most telling original contribution was the concept of elasticity we looked at closely on Wednesday. He's also known as the person who taught Keynes economics.

- **John Maynard Keynes (1883–1946)**: The greatest economist of the twentieth century, Keynes created the subject of macroeconomics, outlined in his *General Theory of Employment, Interest and Money* published in 1936. Since the 1930s he has defined the debate about how economists think about the economy, whether you agree with him or not. His ideas had a 'good' financial crisis after 2008.

- **Joan Robinson (1903–83)**: A rare eminent female economist, but let's hope not the last, Robinson should probably have been awarded a Nobel Prize in Economics for her work on monopolistic competition alone. As a student and disciple of Keynes, she was important in promoting his ideas after the 'General Theory' was published.

- **Ronald Coase (1910–2013)**: His 1937 paper *The Nature of the Firm* introduced the notion that market transaction costs create a need to have businesses. Coase's ideas continue to dominate economists' thinking on business. He is also famous for his Coase theorem, which suggests that allocating property rights can solve problems caused by negative externalities.

- **Milton Friedman (1912–2006)**: Friedman advocated markets at every opportunity. He thought businesses should concentrate on making profits and not solving social problems. Best known, and highly influential in his lifetime, for an updated version of the Quantity Theory of Money, he thought controlling the money supply would control inflation. In later life, he recanted this view.

- **Oliver Williamson (1932–)**: A student of Coase, Williamson has developed the notion that transaction costs determine when businesses should be formed. He has much to say about whether businesses should constantly renegotiate contracts with suppliers and contractors or develop longer-term relationships with them that avoid the continuing costs of negotiation, an important transaction cost.

5 Seven everyday economic misunderstandings

- **There's only so much work that needs doing in a society.** See the discussion of 'infinite wants' in Sunday's chapter for a refutation of this suggestion.
- **Trade is a competition.** No, it's not. Done right, it's a mutually beneficial activity.
- **Markets encourage selfish behaviour.** Not so: they allow people to pursue their own interests. These can be generous as well as selfish.
- **Markets are always best for society.** If they fail, they're not.
- **Governments should always balance their books.** Not if they want to boost demand when the economy's in recession, or damp it down in a boom. These are vital tasks that government can perform for the economy.
- **Businesses create jobs.** On the contrary: consumers are the source of jobs when they demand the goods businesses produce. Businesses respond to this demand.
- **Labour-saving technology causes unemployment.** Wrong: other things cause unemployment. Workers who lose jobs

should find work elsewhere if the economy's running smoothly. Infinite wants guarantee that there will always be work to be done.

6 Seven economic ideas to savour

- People pursue their own interests in markets. But markets ensure that the result is what's best for society. It's a wonderful paradox and it applies as long as markets don't fail.
- Prices allocate scarce resources without the expense of employing government officials, administrators or planners. It all happens invisibly.
- Businesses shouldn't always charge their customers the same price. They can make more profit charging some of them different prices. It's the demand curve.
- Unemployment is not inevitable. Infinite wants see to that. As does...
- ...Comparative advantage, which means everybody can play a role in the economy, however limited their abilities.
- New technology raises output, makes more of scarce resources, and might even make the world a better place. It's not a threat.
- 'Money makes the world go around'. It's a song title that captures a crucial idea: money makes exchanging goods, and so satisfying wants, much easier.

7 Seven songs for economists

- **'You Can't Always Get What You Want' – The Rolling Stones** Everything you needed to know about economics in a song title. Coupled with '(I Can't Get No) Satisfaction', it shows the obvious influence studying economics had on Mick Jagger's songwriting.
- **'Supply and Demand' – The Hives** A surprisingly large number of songs take this most economics of titles. So if

this is too raucous for you – and it might be – others with the same title are available.

- **'Bills, Bills, Bills' – Destiny's Child** In market economies, the benefits of consuming come with responsibilities. You have to produce to pay those bills. Free ride too much and other participants in the market don't like it. It's a message straight from the heart of economics.

- **'Price Tag' – Jessie J** A reminder that there's more to life than the price tag. Economists would agree! It's not about the money; it's about satisfaction. But if the economy's broken, it's a lot harder to have 'a good time' than when it's working well. Not so good on economics, then, but makes the world dance.

- **'Money' – The Flying Lizards** The vast number of songs with the word money in the title shows how central it is to human societies. This one is almost randomly chosen from among them. But, despite that, a worthy version of the classic paean of praise to money and infinite wants.

- **'No Banker Left Behind' – Ry Cooder** Probably the best song about the 2008 financial crisis. It puts the blame for the crisis where many economists would put it.

- **'Them Belly Full (But We Hungry)' – Bob Marley and the Wailers** Allocation of resources raises more than just economic issues. Bob Marley portrays possible consequences of inequality. The version on the album *Live!* is the best.

Answers

Sunday: 1b; 2c; 3d; 4c; 5a; 6a; 7b; 8c; 9d; 10b

Monday: 1c; 2a; 3d; 4b; 5c; 6b; 7d 8b; 9b; 10c

Tuesday: 1d; 2a; 3c; 4d; 5d; 6c; 7b; 8b; 9c; 10a

Wednesday: 1b; 2d; 3c; 4a; 5c; 6d; 7d; 8b; 9d; 10a

Thursday: 1b; 2a; 3c; 4c; 5d; 6a; 7c; 8d; 9b; 10b

Friday: 1a; 2a; 3b; 4d; 5c; 6a; 7b; 8b; 9a; 10d

Saturday: 1a; 2b; 3b; 4d; 5a; 6d; 7b; 8c; 9a; 10b